Camping
South Carolina

Melissa Watson

GUILFORD, CONNECTICUT
HELENA, MONTANA
AN IMPRINT OF GLOBE PEQUOT PRESS

To buy books in quantity for corporate use
or incentives, call **(800) 962-0973**
or e-mail **premiums@GlobePequot.com**.

FALCONGUIDES®

FalconGuides is an imprint of Globe Pequot Press.
Falcon, FalconGuides, and Outfit Your Mind are registered trademarks of Morris Book Publishing, LLC.

Maps: created by Mapping Specialists Ltd. © Morris Book Publishing LLC.

Project editor: Lauren Szalkiewicz
Layout: Sue Murray
Interior photos by Melissa Watson

Library of Congress Cataloging-in-Publication Data is available on file.

ISBN 978-0-7627-8436-3

Printed in the United States of America

10 9 8 7 6 5 4 3 2 1

For my nieces & nephews!
Christina & Cory Payton.
Frank, Thomas, Joe, Kristen, Rebecca, & Nathaniel Strazza.
Michelle Arisolo.
You've brought me so much joy!
From the moment you were born to this very day, I am thankful to
be blessed with such a perfect bunch!
I love you all!
xoxo
—From your favorite aunt!

Contents

Overview

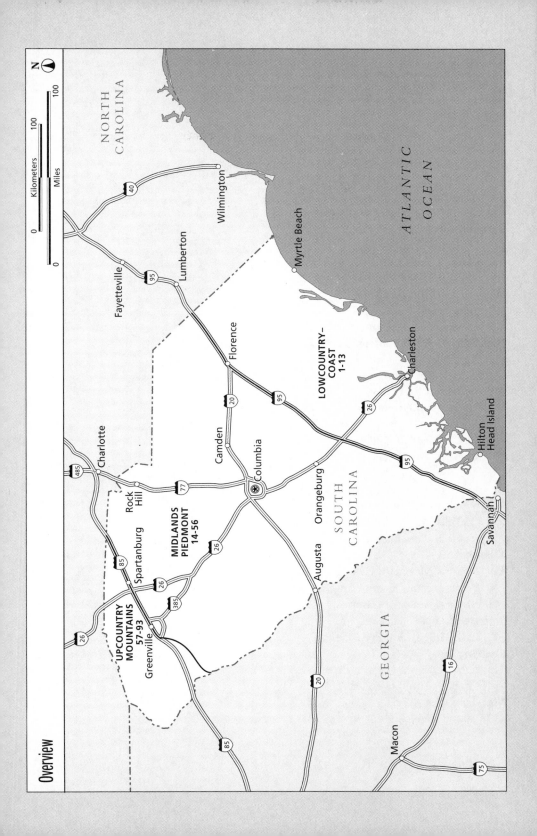

N

NORTH CAROLINA

ATLANTIC OCEAN

SOUTH CAROLINA

GEORGIA

Kilometers
0   100
Miles
0   100

UPCOUNTRY MOUNTAINS 57-93

MIDLANDS PIEDMONT 14-56

LOWCOUNTRY-COAST 1-13

Wilmington

Fayetteville

Lumberton

Myrtle Beach

Florence

Charlotte

Camden

Columbia

Rock Hill

Spartanburg

Orangeburg

Greenville

Augusta

Charleston

Hilton Head Island

Savannah

Macon

40

95

20

26

77

485

85

385

16

75

Acknowledgments

First and foremost, my entire family has been so supportive in every way! Terri San-sonetti, Maria, Frazier, Christina and Cory Payton, Doug Watson, Sue, Tom, Frank, Amy, Thomas, Luana, Joe, Dena, Kristen, Rebecca, Nathaniel, Katilee, Mark, Jonathon and Joshua, and Silas Strazza, Michelle, Roland and Lucas Arisolo, Doug and Clare Watson. I love you all! Thank you!

To my "besties": Dawn McKinney, Shari Santos, Jenn Getter, Cheryl Giovagno-rio, Liz Martinez, Irene Freer, Terri Bennett, Kenisha Wiggins—thanks for filling my down time with laughter, love, and lots of fun! I love you all—you are my extended family!

As always, my crew at Station 51—Craig Hatton, Chris Uzzo, Scott Barksdale, David Adams, and Mike Osuna . . . We mesh . . . On calls, in training, around the station. So much laughter, so many good times. I wouldn't trade you guys for the world! And to you, Amy Kott—you braved it out for two weeks in a tent, with a hundred-pound dog to boot. You saw the best and the worst of South Carolina's campgrounds. You wore many hats—driver, scribe, camp cook, etc.

And, although you fought me every morning at 6 a.m. rise time, you made this road trip far more enjoyable! We covered a lot of ground, and through it all, you were a real trooper and a phenomenal help! Thank you, Amy!

As for the folks associated with the parks and national forests, you were an integral part of assuring accuracy. In particular: Debbie Laughridge, Michael Reid, Susan Spell, Russ Stock, Zabo McCants, Butch Diggers, Barbara Smith, James Thompson, Joetta Harrell, Daniel Gambrell, Pamela Jackson, Joanna Stevens, David Senter, Ken McRae, Tony Rivers, Harry Hafer, George Rambo, Fayette Yenny, Todd Rexode, Dee Stiffler, Gerdi Lake, John Wells, Peggy Washko, Mandy Holbrook, Arline Learst, Roy (Rec) Cobb, Brenda Majors, David Collins, Eddie Richburg, Gina Davis, David Drake, Robert Dinkins, Sgt. Ron L. Hedden, James Thompson, David Collins, Larry Bonds, Kim Smith, Kim Baumann, Cindy Wells, Jennifer Majors, Rhonda Griffith, Laura Kirk, Kenny Boggs, Steve Holstetler, Roni Wenstrom, David Finney, Curry Murray, Stacey Leopard, Noel Simons, Brian Lacy, James Lyles, John Wells, Laura Led-ford, Raegan Ashley, Lindsey Brown, Karen Merchant, Glen Kansanback, Kyle Bull-ock, Nathan Dinehart and the staff at the Army Corps of Engineers-Lake Hartwell, Cory at Kings Mountain State Park, the staff at Jones Gap State Park, Brooks Garrett, James Christie, John Moon, Eddie Richburg, Jawana Stephens, Alice Riddle, Mandy Holbrook, Randy McCoy, and Gwyn Ingram—thank you.

Introduction

South Carolina, the belle of the south. Nearly surrounded by water, to the west the entire Georgia/South Carolina state line is composed of rivers, and to the east lies the Atlantic Ocean, spanning the entire coastline. Whether you sat in traffic for hours to get here, or if you just popped into town to stay at the local neighborhood campground, at the end of the day it's all the same. It's all about the peace of the forest, the tranquility of a clear mountain lake, or the sound of the river rushing by. It's about the simple serenity of just getting away from it all. As you listen to the crickets and the crackle of the fire, the stress unfolds, unravels, and unwinds. And now, you know why you're here, camping in South Carolina. From the far southern reaches of Hunting Island State Park, to the mountains of the Upcountry and everything in between. Creeks and waterfalls, lakes and forest, from endless mountain views to the fresh salty air of the infinite ocean, South Carolina has it all!

No matter what your style of camping, whether you string a hammock between two trees and sleep under the stars, or if you prefer the creature comforts of an RV, South Carolina has a place for you. Mikey, my 100-pound puppy, and I spent months in a tent exploring every corner and every public campground and "primitive campsite" in the state—this time with a little twist. A dear friend of mine joined us for part of the adventure. While I usually travel solo with Mikey at my side, I must admit the company was a welcome addition, not to mention an amazing help setting up camp and gathering information. All this time on the road, and Mikey still can't set up a tent. Exhausting research went into compiling data, both online and on the phone, before and after each road trip. In doing my homework, we drove thousands of miles, gathering the facts, exploring in person, and trying to get you as much accurate information as humanly possible. I hope my efforts shine brightly through these pages.

The main focus of this book is campgrounds that you can drive right up to, put the car in park, and set up camp. I have also included a few campgrounds that require a short walk/hike to reach. I've done my very best to provide you with as much information as possible, but I still recommend that you stop by the ranger station or visitor's center whenever possible before setting up camp. These folks are full of knowledge and an amazing asset. Not only that, they are kind, caring, and more than happy to help in any way they can. Pack your gear, load the car, grab your camera, and get out and explore!

How to Use This Guide

As you thumb through the pages of this book, you will notice that it's been broken down into geographic regions. For simplicity's sake, I have opted to use the three major regions commonly used in the state of South Carolina: The Lowcountry or coastal region, the Midlands or Piedmont region, and the Upcountry or mountain region. To help you navigate and find the campground nearest your destination, I have broken the regions down further into even smaller geographic areas, based on the nearest town. Maps are provided for each area, and tables are a useful tool for a quick reference to see if a campground suits your needs. For each entry I have provided essential information on certain common elements. Here's a brief explanation of each.

Location: If applicable, I have provided a physical address, and the distance and direction from nearby towns to help you get a general idea of where the campground is.

Season: While many of the campgrounds in the coastal region are open year-round, some, in the mountain region in particular, may only be open seasonally. I have listed the season dates, but some are subject to change. It's always a good idea to call first and confirm that they are open and that campsites are available, especially in the winter months from November to March.

Sites: Here, I have listed the number and type of campsites available. RV sites can accommodate RVs and may or may not have electric and water hookups. Tent sites are designed specifically for tent camping, but you can still drive right up to your site. Walk-in/canoe-to campsites are tent only, and require that you either walk in a short distance, or boat to the campsites. For those of you looking for a less rustic experience, some of the campgrounds offer cabin rentals as well. Group camps and group camping areas listed in this guide are typically reserved for nonprofit organizations, such as the Boy or Girl Scouts, or church groups, but often times, the campgrounds have been known to make exceptions on this. So, if you are planning a trip with seventeen of your closest friends, the logistics are much easier if you can simply stay in a group campsite, and it certainly doesn't hurt to ask. Many of the campgrounds in this guide, and every state park in South Carolina, offer a limited number of wheelchair-accessible campsites. If you are in need of these sites, please contact the campground directly to check for availability.

Maximum length: Is just that, the maximum-length RV that the campground can accommodate. Not to be confused with the maximum length of stay, which, in most places, is 14 days. The majority of campgrounds in this book can fit up to 40-foot RVs, and some can handle RVs as big as 109 feet. Often, however, there are a limited number of campsites that can fit extremely long RVs. If you have an oversize RV, it's a good idea to check with the campground ahead of time to make sure they have a site available that can accommodate you.

Facilities: What's available at the campground? Whether the bathhouse has flush or vault toilets, and if you can expect a hot shower or not. Is there a camp store, or any other traditional amenities, such as a picnic table or fire ring? In all cases where I state that a campground has electric available, I am referring to 30 amp service. If you require 50 amp service, contact the park directly to check for availability.

Fee: I personally visited every campground in this book in 2013. The fees listed are per night and based on what the fee was at that time. As with anything in life, fees do go up over the years.

$ = $0–$10

$$ = $10–$19

$$$ = $20 or more

If you see a range of fees such as $$–$$$, assume that the tent sites are less and the RV sites cost more. Many of the campgrounds have what's known as a self-pay station at the entrance. At these self-pay stations, it's based on the honor system. You fill out an envelope, place the fee inside, drop it in the safe box, and you are good to go. Keep in mind, you will need exact change, unless you don't mind donating a few extra dollars to the forest service.

The National Forest Service also offers "Interagency Senior Passes" for a nominal fee ($$). Pass holders receive a discount of 50 percent at many National Forest campgrounds, and on other extended amenity fees. To obtain a senior pass, you must be at least 62 years of age, and you must apply for the pass in person. Passes are available at most national forest offices, but I recommend you call ahead, just in case. The state park service also offers an annual park "passport," but this passport is available to everyone, not just for seniors. These state park passes can be purchased online and grant the pass holder free entry to the state parks, plus other perks and privileges. To get yours now, or for more information, visit their website at www .southcarolinaparks.com/park-passport/default.aspx.

Management: I have gone to great lengths to try to include every public campground in the state. With that in mind, "management" lists the agency that maintains the park, whether it be local, state, or federal.

Contact: Here I have listed the phone number and any pertinent websites where you can obtain more information. If a campground takes reservations, often times there is a separate phone number or website for that, so I have included this information under the contact heading as well. Keep in mind, many of the campgrounds fill up quickly, especially on weekends and holidays. It's a good idea to take advantage of the reservation system to assure you get a campsite.

Finding the campground: I've given my best effort to provide you with explicit driving directions, but there is nothing more valuable than a good map to help you navigate. I highly recommend the *DeLorme: South Carolina Atlas and Gazetteer*. I have been using this, in conjunction with the National Geographic topographical maps, for years. I must say that these maps have been an invaluable tool when finding my way around the mountains and back roads across the state. They include highways, state roads, and many forest service roads as well. So many people rely strongly on GPS units nowadays, or on maps in their "smart" phones. While these do hold some value, I cannot stress enough that they also have their limitations. A GPS is only as good as its signal, and a "smart" phone is only useful when you have a signal. Please be aware that in many areas of the national forest, and in remote parts of the state, you will not have cell phone service. So be sure to have a map handy as a backup plan.

GPS coordinates: As stated above, more and more people are using GPS units to navigate. For this reason, I have included GPS coordinates for each campground entry.

About the campground: Just as you would expect, this is where I tell you a little bit about the campground, and what to expect when you visit. Along with a description, this is where I will tell you what kind of activities the campground offers, such as hiking, mountain biking, etc. I also alert you to any nearby attractions that may catch your attention while you're in the area.

The majority of entries in this guide are your traditional campgrounds that welcome RVs, pop-ups, and tent campers. But in my effort to include every public campground in the state, I have also included a few different types of campgrounds as well. For instance:

Horse camps: You'll find a few of these within these pages, and they are just that. They are designed with the equestrian community in mind. They may have corrals or stables to house your horse, or even a horse washing station or a manure bin on-site. This is not to say that individuals without horses can't camp here; it's simply that these campgrounds offer a place for the equestrian community to camp with their horse right alongside them.

Backcountry campgrounds: There are only two true backcountry campgrounds included here: Jones Gap State Park and Burrells Ford Campground. First off, the impeccable quality of the camping experience at these two campgrounds has led me to include them, despite the fact that this is not necessarily a backcountry camping guide. A short hike from a few hundred feet to about a half a mile will lead you to these picture-perfect primitive campsites. Be advised that when backcountry camping, you can only access the campsites by foot, and you must carry all your gear into and back out of your campsite. I urge you to practice "leave no trace" camping principles and pack it in, pack it out.

Primitive campsites: The upcountry of South Carolina, in particular the Andrew Pickens district of the Sumter National Forest, has an astounding number of "primitive campsites." These sites are typically a single campsite, although a few do have a handful of campsites at the same location. For specific information read each individual entry, but in general, you can drive right up to these primitive sites and set up camp (usually down a bumpy, dirt forest service road). They are designed for tent camping, although you can set an RV up at some of them. But the most important thing to know is that these sites are truly primitive, meaning there are few or no amenities. The most to expect is a vault toilet, certainly no showers, water, or electric, and most only have a stone fire ring to adorn them. Usually, the campsite will have a brown carbonite sign that reads CAMPING PERMITTED BEHIND THIS SIGN. This is the only indication that you have arrived at the designated primitive campsite, so pay close attention to my specific driving directions. As rustic and primal as they are, surprisingly, they actually see a lot of traffic and are often occupied, especially on the weekends. When you camp at these sites, remember to bring all your supplies, food, and lots of water. Don't forget a shovel to dig a cat hole for a bathroom, and please remember to clean up after yourself when you vacate the campsite. The next camper certainly doesn't want to find the trash you left behind when they arrive. Leave no trace, and pack it in, pack it out.

Key for Tables:
Total sites
Hookup sites
Maximum RV length: In feet
Hookups: E=Electric, W=Water, S=Sewer
Toilets: F=Flush, V=Vault
Showers: Y or N
Drinking water: Y or N
Dump station: Y or N
Recreation:
    H=Hiking
    S=Swimming
    F=Fishing
    B=Boating
    L=Boat launch
    R=Horseback riding/bridle trails
    M=Mountain biking
    C=Cycling
    O=Off-highway vehicle trails (OHV)
    A=Archery
    BB=Basketball
    T=Tennis
    Tu=Tubing
    V=Volleyball
    G=Golf
    DG=Disc golf
    MG=Mini golf
    HS=Horseshoe pits
    P=Picnicking
    ★★=Other activities
Fee: $, $$, $$$
Reservations: Y or N

For Your Safety

Whenever you are planning a camping trip, whether you'll be sleeping in a tent or housed in an RV, there are always certain preparations that need to be made and important things to consider. Here are a few friendly reminders to help you enjoy your camping experience to the fullest.

Weather: The weather in South Carolina can range from hot, hot, hot on the coast in the summer to snow on the mountains in the winter. Do your homework before you go, and remember to dress in layers. This way, you can be prepared for any fluctuations that Mother Nature may throw at you, and always have your rain gear handy just in case.

Clothing: A few items that I find very useful are zip-off pants and wool socks. The pants are great because they are thin but still keep you warm, and they double as shorts simply by zipping off the legs. As for the wool socks, there's no better way to stay warm in a tent at night then a good pair (or two) of wool socks. There's a funny saying: "cotton kills," and there is some truth to this. If you run, hike, or bike in cotton, or get stuck in the rain, once cotton gets wet, it stays wet, keeping your body temperature dangerously low in cold weather. Wool, on the other hand, retains heat. I also recommend the new "technical" quick-dry materials; they are fantastic for their moisture-wicking ability. Last, if you plan on hiking or even mountain biking during hunting season, always be aware of your surroundings, and wear blaze orange to make yourself clearly visible. Big game and turkey hunting season is usually mid-September to January 4 and late March to May 3 in South Carolina, but do your homework, and check for specific dates before you go.

Gear: I don't care how experienced you are. Even if you've camped a thousand times or so, for some reason the fates always toy with us when it comes time to pack our gear. Sure enough, you're bound to forget one thing or another; it never fails. So, follow Santa's practice of making a list and checking it twice, then check your gear twice too. There's nothing worse than being starving after a long day on the trail, and then realizing you forgot a can opener or a lighter to light your stove and campfire. I guess that bowl of warm chili on a cold night that you were so looking forward to will just have to wait.

Here are a few sundry items that are always good to bring along: A foldable camp chair for sitting and reading by the campfire is essential. If you're in a tent, a tarp for under your tent helps keep out the dampness from the ground, and sometimes a tarp on top helps if you are in torrential downpours (even if you've sprayed your tent with "camp dry") or simply gives you a little shade in the heat of summer. The last item that I really do not leave home without is a pack towel. These chamois-type towels are super lightweight, they pack up to be very small, and they dry in minutes by simply hanging them out, or laying them on a rock for a few minutes in the sun. You can find them at local outfitters or in camping outlets like REI.

Many of the campgrounds are deep within the forest, in very remote areas that are far from towns, hospitals, and civilization. This may be part of why you came here in the first place. But there is some risk associated with this isolation. You may not have a cell phone signal, so it's a good idea to bring a first-aid kit and plenty of food and water, and if you're in an RV, gas up when you can. Always give someone your itinerary before heading out, and let them know when you are expected to return as well.

Firearms and alcohol: No, not together! Ever! That would make for a horrible combination with most likely dire consequences. I simply grouped them, because both firearms and alcohol are prohibited in all the state parks and county parks in this guidebook.

Water: If for any reason you need to drink water from a creek, find a strong flowing creek, and be sure to treat or filter the water. Many animals drink from the streams, and at times they use it as a bathroom. Keep in mind that even the clearest creek or river still carries tiny bacteria and parasites in it.

Fish: Some, certainly not all, fish caught in South Carolina may contain harmful levels of mercury. For more information, visit the Fish Advisory website at www.scd hec.gov/fish or call (888) 849-7241. While we are on the subject of fish, be advised that nearly every place that allows fishing in this guidebook requires you to first obtain a South Carolina state fishing license. Licenses can be purchased at a few of the campgrounds listed, or you can plan ahead and get one online at www.dnr.sc.gov/purchase.html. Many of the state parks in this guide participate in a tackle loaner program that is sponsored by the South Carolina Department of Natural Resources. This program allows you to borrow/check out fishing equipment from the park office. Inquire at each individual campground to see if they participate, and remember, you still need to have your own state fishing license before you cast your line.

Poison ivy, oak, and sumac: All three of these plant irritants are common in the forests of South Carolina. If you do your homework ahead of time and know how to identify them, you may save yourself some unpleasant itching. A nice little rule of thumb is "leaves of three, let it be," since poison ivy and oak both typically have three leaflets to a leaf.

Bugs, bees, and ticks: Whether you have known allergies or not, it's a *very* good idea to carry Benadryl with you at all times. While hiking deep in the forest with Mikey one time, we were viciously attacked by an angry swarm of bees. I have never been allergic to bees in my life, but the stings were so numerous that I literally started to feel a lump in my throat as my airway began to swell shut. I am a professional paramedic. This is not an exaggeration. I truly believe I may not be alive right now if I did not have Benadryl in my pack for both Mikey and me. If you have known allergies, an EpiPen is essential. As much as I hate to condone it, insect repellant is sometimes a must to keep the bugs away, especially in the early evening hours of the hot summer months. Bug spray containing DEET seems to deter both mosquitoes and ticks. As for the ticks, these heat-seeking parasites are sneaky little buggers, and unfortunately they are quite prevalent throughout the state. It's a good idea to do a thorough "tick check" each night when you take a shower or before you go to bed. You may not even feel a tiny tick embedding himself under your skin. If you do find a tick on you, tweezers work well for removing them, and they also make a tool designed specifically for tick removal, which is available for sale at some of the campground camp stores.

Courtesy: People camp for the peace and quiet. They do not want to hear you blaring your favorite song on the radio. Show your neighbors a little courtesy, and remember quiet hours are typically from 10 p.m. to 6 a.m.

Pets: I'm a big fan of dogs and animals in general. As a matter of fact, my big dog Mikey spent the night in a tent with me at almost every campground in this book. But, as a person camping with a pet, you must be mindful. Not everyone loves your furry friends as much as you do. So keep them on a leash at all times. Again, be courteous, especially if they tend to be vocal, and always pick up after them.

For Mother Nature's Safety

Wildlife: When you are out in the forest, you are a guest in the forest. Remember, many animals make their home here. Some you may not like, such as snakes and spiders, and others are cute and furry like otters and beavers. No matter what you come across, whether it's a squirrel, a deer, or a bear, please DO NOT feed wildlife. Often these cuddly critters cannot digest people food, so you may be doing them more harm than good. More importantly, in the case of bears, for instance, the bear will then associate people with food. This inadvertently makes him a "nuisance" bear. There is a very sad, but true saying, "a fed bear is a dead bear," because they will euthanize a nuisance bear to protect the public. Please do not contribute to this. Instead, help keep wildlife wild.

Campfires: Campfires are one of the many reasons people enjoy camping. It offers you a place to gather with your loved ones and roast marshmallows, or to tell scary ghost stories, or simply sit and enjoy the flicker of the flames as you listen to the sounds of nature. Please be responsible with your fire. You don't need a massive bonfire to appreciate its warmth and beauty. Always make sure that your campfire is completely out prior to vacating your campsite. Do not burn trash. If you collect wood from the forest, only collect felled wood. Never cut live trees or brush to use as firewood. For one thing, you are killing the tree, and secondly, green wood does not burn, it smolders. All you will be doing is making an annoyingly smoky fire. Many of the campgrounds sell firewood. I urge you to use the wood provided by the campground rather than bring your own. Bringing in your own firewood may also bring in some invasive species that are making their home in your bundle of wood. You may inadvertently introduce those nonnative invasive species into the forest simply by bringing in your own firewood.

Keep a clean camp: For a number of reasons. Number one, littering is just bad. Plain and simple. The next people to camp at your site do not want to have to pick up your cigarette butt or bottle cap. Please use a trash bag and do not leave it out at night. Raccoons, opossums, and skunks love to rummage for food in the darkness of the night. What better an easy target than some unsuspecting camper's trash?

Food storage: Those same critters that like your trash love your food. I swear raccoons must have opposable thumbs. They can get into just about anything. As for black bears, they do inhabit South Carolina. So be sure to stow your food away properly, keeping it in your car or RV at night. If you are sleeping in a tent, and do not have a car with you, bring plenty of rope along to string your food and trash up in between trees. Never bring food into your tent in bear country!

Dishes and cat holes: Wash any dishes well away from any natural water source. On a similar and more important note, if no bathrooms are provided, and you must go in the forest, dig a "cat hole" to bury your waste at least 200 feet from any creek, river, lake, etc.

Leave NO Trace: The last thing I'd like to share with you is a concept known as Leave No Trace camping. Simply put, when you leave, it should be just as you arrived (if not cleaner). "Take nothing but pictures, leave nothing but footprints." At times, you will hear me refer to "pack it in, pack it out." This means everything you bring into the forest, you should also bring out of the forest, leaving no trace, and no sign that you were ever there. This leaves less impact on the environment, and allows other campers to appreciate the natural beauty of their surroundings.

Author's Favorites

1   Hunting Island State Park
11   Myrtle Beach State Park
13   Little Pee Dee State Park
14   Cheraw State Park
30   Modoc Campground
31   Hamilton Branch State Park
32   Hawe Creek Campground
37   Mt. Carmel Campground
59   Jones Gap State Park
62   Devil's Fork State Park
63   Mile Creek County Park
67   Clemson University's Eagle's Nest Tree House
71   Sadlers Creek State Park
72   Crescent Group Camp
93   Burrells Ford Backcountry Campground

Map Legend

Transportation

≡(95)≡   Interstate Highway

≡(1)≡   US Highway

≡(161)≡   State Highway

≡[33]≡   Other State Road

≡≡≡   Local Road

= = = =   Unpaved Road

Land Management

▭   National Park/Forest

▭   State/County Park/Forest

Symbols

●   Campground

✪   Capital

○   City/Town

❓   Visitor Center

■   Point of Interest

Water Features

⬭   Body of Water

〰   River/Creek

Lowcountry–Coast

With merely a baker's dozen of public campgrounds spanning the entire coastal region, you may have to travel a bit farther to reach your destination. But although they are few and somewhat far between, these campgrounds pack a punch! It's not often that you can camp just yards away from the ocean shore, wake up in the morning, and pop off for a swim as the sun rises over the deep blue sea.

Yet opportunity after opportunity presents itself with beachside camping alongside the Atlantic Ocean in the Lowcountry of South Carolina. As a matter of fact, nearly half of the coastal campgrounds are within easy reach of the beach. As you sit by the fire at these waterfront wonderlands, your tensions are eased by the flicker of the flames. Soon, your stress slips away as the sound of the waves lapping on the sand slowly soothes your soul. From the far southern reaches of Hunting Island, to world-class golf in Myrtle Beach. The pristine water of Lake Moultrie and Marion, and the Great Pee Dee River Basin. From the Grand Strand in the north, to the fishing wharves of Beaufort in the south. Enjoy trails of every kind in Francis Marion National Forest as they pass through the long leaf pines. Sightsee in historic Charleston or enjoy freshly caught seafood in Murrells Inlet. Whatever you fancy, it's yours to embrace, here along the breathtaking coast of South Carolina.

Splendid views of the Atlantic Ocean await.

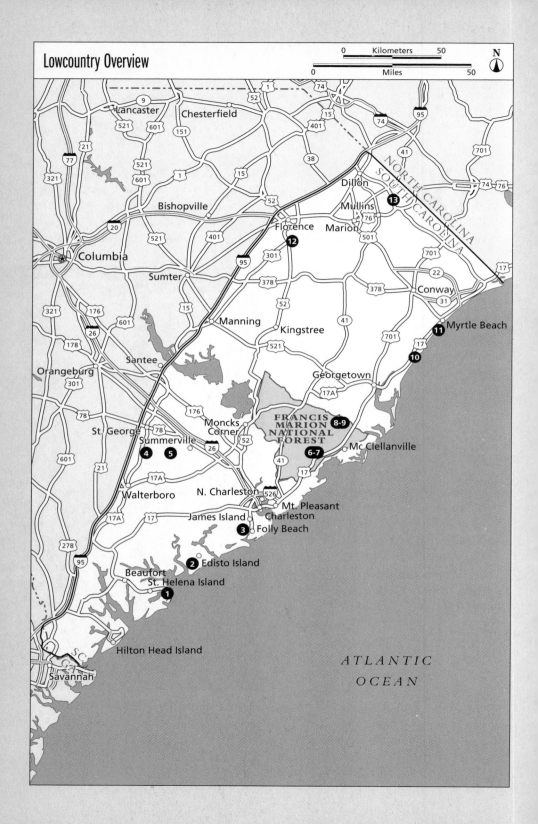

Lowcountry Overview

Beaufort Area

Campground	Total sites	Hookup sites	Max. RV length	Hookups	Toilets	Showers	Drinking water	Dump station	Recreation	Fee	Reservations
1 Hunting Island State Park	213	167	45'	E, W	F	Y	Y	Y	H, M, R*, S, F, B, L, V, P	$$-$$$	Y

* See campground entry for specific information

1 Hunting Island State Park

Location: 2555 Sea Island Pkwy., Hunting Island, about 17 miles east of Port Royal
Season: Year-round
Sites: 210; 3 group campsites are also available and can accommodate up to 30 people each
Maximum length: 45 feet
Facilities: Flush toilets, hot showers, electric, water, water spigots dispersed (tent sites only), fire rings, picnic tables, lantern holders, dump station, ice and firewood for sale, sandy beach, pet friendly
Fee per night: $$-$$$
Management: South Carolina Department of Natural Resources
Contact: (843) 838-2011; www.southcarolinaparks .com/huntingisland/camping.aspx; for reservations call (866) 345-7275 or visit www.reserve america.com
Finding the campground: From the junction of US 21 and SC 802 East in Beaufort, drive east on US 21 for 14.0 miles to a left onto Campground Road (SR 348) at the entrance to the campground.

From I-95 get off at exit 33 and drive east on US 17 for 8.3 miles to a right onto US 21 South toward Beaufort. Follow US 21 for 31.4 miles to the entrance to the campground on the left.
GPS coordinates: N32 23.204 / W80 25.961
Maps: *DeLorme: South Carolina Atlas and Gazetteer* page 63, A10
About the campground: Diversity is at its best in this oceanfront campground, resting along the shores of the Atlantic. Pine and oak trees live hand in hand with the palms and palmettos, and there's

The Hunting Island Lighthouse towers above.

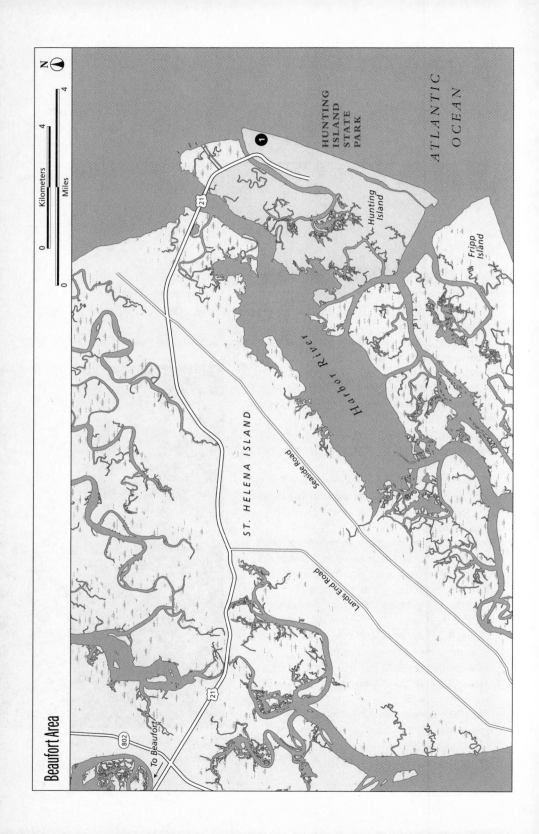

Beaufort Area

N

Kilometers
0   4

Miles
0   4

To Beaufort

802

21

ST. HELENA ISLAND

Seaside Road

Lands End Road

21

Harbor River

Hunting
Island

Fripp
Island

HUNTING
ISLAND
STATE
PARK

1

ATLANTIC
OCEAN

Fishermen thrive in the coastal region of South Carolina.

a surprisingly abundant amount of bird life. From cardinals to woodpeckers, brilliantly colored painted buntings and tanagers alike can be found flying about the tree cover of Hunting Island. A marsh boardwalk and hiking and bike trails traverse the park. With a fishing pier, two boat ramps, the beach, and a lighthouse to boot, this park gets the highest marks from me. A South Carolina state fishing license is not required to fish from the pier, but you must have one to fish anywhere else in the park. During the winter months the beach is open for equestrian use as well, but you must obtain a permit first. Although it does see a lot of traffic, and the campsites are a bit over-crowded, the ambiance of the ocean overshadows any downfall. Some of the sites sit as close as 50 yards from the surf, and as you rest your head upon the pillow at night, the waves lapping upon the shore lull you to sleep.

Charleston Area

Campground	Total sites	Hookup sites	Max. RV length	Hookups	Toilets	Showers	Drinking water	Dump station	Recreation	Fee	Reservations
2a **Edisto Beach State Park–Live Oak Campground**	53	48	60'	E, W	F	Y	Y	Y	H, M, S, F, B, L, V, G*, P	$$–$$$	Y
2b **Edisto Beach State Park–Beach Campground**	64	64	75'	E, W	F	Y	Y	Y	H, M, S, F, B, L, V, G*, P	$$–$$$	Y
3 **James Island County Park**	164	124	109'	E, W, S*	F	Y	Y	Y	H*, C, S*, F, B*, L*, DG, P, **, Dog Park	$$$	Y

* See campground entry for specific information

2 Edisto Beach State Park

Location: 8377 State Cabin Rd., Edisto Island; about 50 miles southwest of Charleston
Season: Year-round
Sites: 112; 5 walk-in campsites are also available; cabin rentals are also available
Maximum length: 75 feet, but there are a limited number of sites that can accommodate this size RV
Facilities: Flush toilets, hot showers, electric, water, fire rings, picnic tables, dump station, ice and firewood for sale, pet friendly
Fee per night: $$–$$$
Management: South Carolina Department of Natural Resources
Contact: (843) 869-2156; www.southcarolinaparks.com/edistobeach/camping.aspx; for reservations call (866) 345-7275 or visit www.reserveamerica.com
Finding the campground: From the junction of SC 174 and US 17 in Osborn, drive south on SC 174 for 20.9 miles to the entrance to the park on your right.
Note: At 2.5 miles, be sure to stay right, continuing to follow SC 174 south.
GPS coordinates: Beach Campground: N32 30.253 / W80 17.779; Live Oak Campground: N32 30.741 / W80 18.088
Maps: DeLorme: South Carolina Atlas and Gazetteer page 60, G2
About the campground: Well off the beaten path is the remote island town of Edisto Beach. As you make the long drive through the swampy ACE Basin National Wildlife Refuge, it seems isolated, nearly desolate, aside from the many churches or the random house here and there. But once you arrive, you find this sleepy little town is a wonderful vacation destination, where many people come to get away from it all. Named for the famous river that flows to both the north and south of Edisto Island, the Edisto is the longest free-flowing blackwater river in North America. Two campgrounds grace this delightful state park. The Beach Campground doesn't actually sit directly

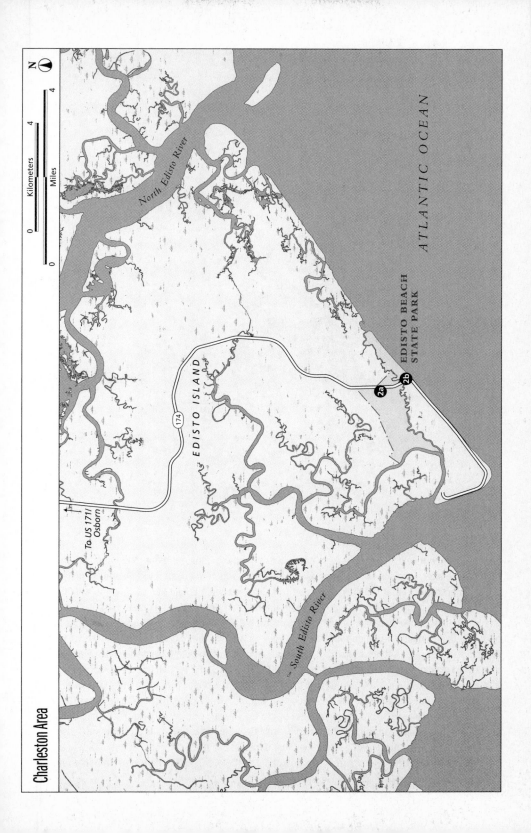

Charleston Area

N

0   4   Kilometers
0   4   Miles

North Edisto River

EDISTO ISLAND

174

To US 17/
Osborn

South Edisto River

EDISTO BEACH
STATE PARK

2a
2b

ATLANTIC OCEAN

Best friends enjoy the ocean view.

on the beach, but several beach access areas lead from the campground out to the sands of the Atlantic. The sites in this family-oriented area of the park are crowded, so if you want a bit more privacy, I recommend that you stay in the Live Oak Campground instead. At Live Oak, you will find deep, wooded campsites that rest alongside the marsh land. The sites are spread out well from one another, but make sure you bring bug spray for the early evening hours. As you explore the park, you find that seashells line the beach, and a wide variety of bird species wade in the water and flit about from tree to tree. The park has hiking and mountain bike trails, volleyball, picnic areas, and playgrounds. And, of course, the beach! Swim, fish, collect shells, run, walk, or wade, whatever you fancy. There's a boat ramp at the west end of the park, so you can bring your own boat and head out and explore. You can head to town and take a kayak tour in the salt marsh, hop on a river cruise, or take a fishing charter out to the Atlantic and try your hand at some deep sea fishing. The aquatic opportunities are endless when camping on Edisto Island. The town also has an 18-hole golf course, and a small museum dedicated to preserving the history of the area. I have one other odd outing for you that's quite unique to the area: the Edisto Island Serpentarium.

Many of the campsites at Edisto Beach State Park offer seclusion.

The facility is located just a few miles north of the park on SC 174. They have inside exhibits and outside gardens, and house alligators, snakes, turtles, and lizards.

3 James Island County Park

Location: 871 Riverland Dr., Charleston
Season: Year-round
Sites: 124; 40 group campsites are also available in the primitive camp area and can accommodate up to 10 people each; cabin rentals are also available
Maximum length: 109 feet, but there are a limited number of sites that can accommodate this size RV
Facilities: Flush toilets, hot showers, electric, water, sewer, fire rings, picnic tables, dump station, ice and firewood for sale, laundry facilities, pet friendly
Fee per night: $$$
Management: Charleston County Parks and Recreation Commission
Contact: (864) 795-4386; www.chascoparks.com/index.aspx?NID=1434
Finding the campground: From the junction of SC 171 (Wesley Drive) and US 17 in Charleston, drive south on SC 171 for 1.1 miles to a right onto SC 700. Follow SC 700 west for 1.5 miles to a left onto Riverland Road at the sign for James Island County Park. Travel for 1.7 miles to the park on the right.

From the junction of SC 171 and SC 30 in James Island, drive south on SC 171 for 1.0 mile to a right onto Camp Road. Follow Camp Road for 0.8 mile to where it ends at Riverland Road. Turn right, and travel for 0.1 mile to the park on the left.
GPS coordinates: N32 44.160 / W79 58.955
Maps: *DeLorme: South Carolina Atlas and Gazetteer* page 61, C6
About the campground: Holy cow! The people of Charleston County are blessed to have such a magnificent park at the ready. The activities seem endless. There's a climbing wall, a slack line, and a ropes course that requires reservations to use. A disc golf course and a paved path that's suitable for biking, walking, or rollerblading runs through the park, and they rent bicycles out or you can bring your own. You can go fishing or crabbing from one of the docks, but you must have a South Carolina state fishing license in your possession. Rent a boat by the hour or half hour, or launch your own canoe or kayak and head out for a paddle. As if this isn't enough, they even have a "Splash Zone" water park on the premises that's open seasonally and requires an additional fee ($-$$). There's also a playground with a spray play area that's free of charge, and is open seasonally as well. James Island is extremely pet friendly and houses the best dog park I've ever seen. The dog park sits along the edge of the lake, so the dogs can play together on land, or take a dip to cool off as need be. Heck, they even sell dog toys in the camp store. Needless to say, Mikey was a happy boy at this one! The park office also offers game rentals for games such as cornhole and ladder golf. If you can't find what you want here at James Island County Park, the town with its namesake has an 18-hole golf course for you to try your hand at. But you're not limited there. The park actually has a shuttle service that takes campers to nearby attractions in downtown Charleston and Folly Beach. This service does cost an additional fee ($$), but I can honestly say there's not another public campground in the state that offers this kind of provision. So, now that you've heard about this astounding local park, on to the campground. There's a primitive camping

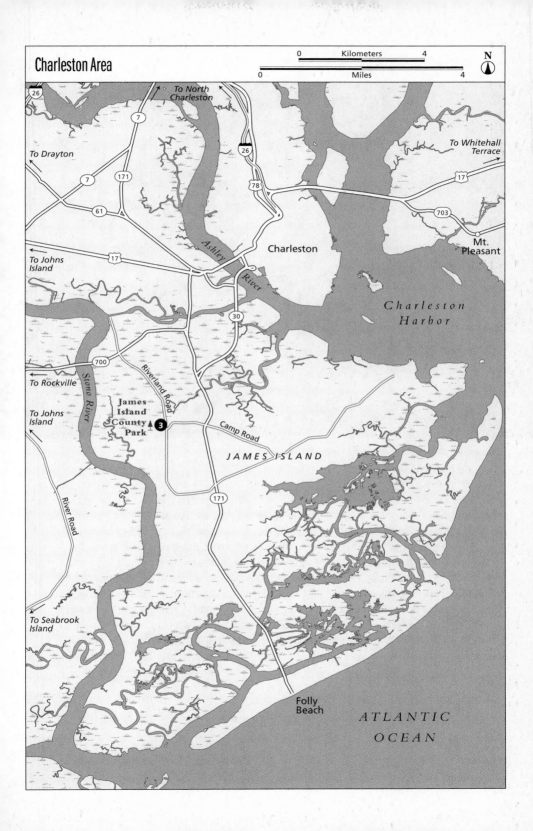

Seashells line the shore along the beaches in Charleston.

area, which really is just an open field. There are no actual designated sites, just several picnic tables scattered about, a fire ring here and there, and a bathhouse. The primitive area is also used for group camping, and there's room for about 40 groups of 10 people per "site." As for the main campground, it's what you would expect of a typical campground. Some of the campsites offer privacy, while many others seem to be on top of each other. I have to say, the park itself, with all its amenities, by far makes up for any downfall that the campground may have. The town of James Island hosts many festivals throughout the year, and the park is home to the annual "Festival of Lights" in November and December, so you may want to call ahead of time to make your reservation and confirm availability. If you're a history buff, I recommend popping up to Mt. Pleasant to the Patriots Point Naval & Maritime Museum. They've got battleships, aircraft, and you can even tour a submarine.

Walterboro Area

Campground	Total sites	Hookup sites	Max. RV length	Hookups	Toilets	Showers	Drinking water	Dump station	Recreation	Fee	Reservations
4 Colleton State Park	27	25	40'	E, W	F	Y	Y	Y	H*, F, B*, L*, V, P	$$	Y
5 Givhans Ferry State Park	26	25	50'	E, W	F	Y	Y	Y	H, M, R*, S, F, B*, L*, V, P	$$	Y

* See campground entry for specific information

4 Colleton State Park

Location: 147 Wayside Lane, Walterboro; about 11 miles north of Walterboro, and about 10 miles south of St. George
Season: Year-round
Sites: 25; 2 group campsites are also available and can accommodate up to 25 people each
Maximum length: 40 feet
Facilities: Flush toilets, hot showers, electric, water, fire rings, picnic tables, dump station, ice and firewood for sale, pet friendly
Fee per night: $$
Management: South Carolina Department of Natural Resources
Contact: (843) 538-8206; www.southcarolinaparks.com/colleton/camping.aspx; for reservations call (866) 345-7275 or visit www.reserveamerica.com
Finding the campground: From I-95 near Walterboro, get off at exit 68, SC 61. Follow SC 61 south for 2.8 miles to a left onto US 15. Follow US 15 north for 0.3 mile to a left onto Wayside Lane at the entrance to the park.
GPS coordinates: N33 03.671 / W80 36.973
Maps: *DeLorme: South Carolina Atlas and Gazetteer* page 54, E2
About the campground: The Edisto River swiftly passes by as it skirts the entire northeastern boundary of the park. A handful of campsites sit above the riverside, giving you a bird's-eye view as it flows downstream. The remainder of sites in the loop are slightly wooded, and not waterfront. The park has a river access point to launch a canoe or kayak, or you can fish from the banks, provided that you have a South Carolina state fishing license. If you don't have your own canoe to launch, you can rent one from the Carolina Heritage Outfitters just north of the park off US 15. There's a large field near the entrance, where you could easily get a game of kickball or football together, and there's also a volleyball net. Take a quick stroll on the 0.3-mile nature trail, or, if you prefer more passive activities, you could head up the road to do some antiquing in the nearby town of Walterboro. Colleton State Park has the traditional group camp area but also allows camping clubs to reserve up to 23 of the regular campsites as well. There's a wonderful recreation building in the campground, but it's only for use by camping clubs and is not open to individual campers. Just minutes from I-95 makes this small state park quite convenient.

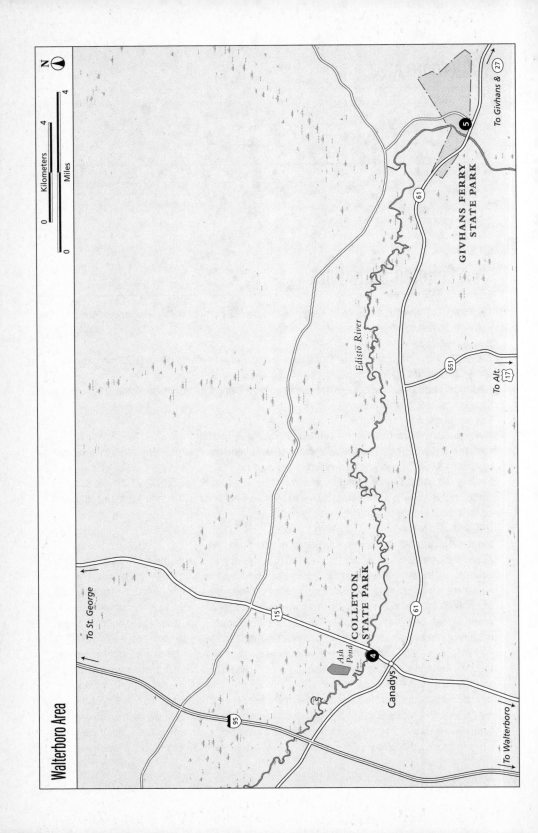

Walterboro Area

N

Kilometers
0   4

Miles
0   4

To St. George

95

15

Ash
Pond

Canadys

COLLETON
STATE PARK

4

Edisto River

61

651

To Alt. 17

GIVHANS FERRY
STATE PARK

5

61

27

To Givhans &

5 Givhans Ferry State Park

Location: 746 Givhans Ferry Rd., Ridgeville; about 20 miles northeast of Walterboro, about 20 miles northeast of North Charleston
Season: Year-round
Sites: 25; 1 group camp area is also available and can accommodate up to 100 people; cabin rentals are also available
Maximum length: 50 feet
Facilities: Flush toilets, hot showers, electric, water, fire rings, picnic tables, dump station, pet friendly
Fee per night: $$
Management: South Carolina Department of Natural Resources
Contact: (843) 873-0692; www.southcarolinaparks.com/givhansferry/camping.aspx; for reservations call (866) 345-7275 or visit www.reserveamerica.com
Finding the campground: From I-95, get off at exit 68 (Canadys exit, SC 61), and follow SC 61 east for 17.2 miles to a left onto Givhans Ferry Road (SR 30) at the sign for Givhans Ferry State Park, and travel for 0.1 mile to the entrance to the park on your left.

From the junction of SC 61 and SC 27 in Givhans, drive west on SC 61 for approximately 3.0 miles to a right onto Givhans Ferry Road and follow the directions above.
GPS coordinates: N33 01.651 / W80 23.137
Maps: *DeLorme: South Carolina Atlas and Gazetteer* page 54, F5
About the campground: At first glance, Givhans Ferry State Park doesn't seem like much. But once you start to explore, you realize that there are quite a few activities offered here. With nearly a thousand acres to its name, the park has hiking and mountain bike trails that are open year-round, and the Old Loop Trail is open for equestrian use on a seasonal basis. The Edisto River skirts the edge of the property, but there's a chain-link fence separating you from the river throughout the park with the exception of one small access area near the park office. It's here that you can launch a canoe or kayak, take a dip, or cast a fishing line, provided you have a South Carolina state fishing license. You can't see the river from the campground, but tree lines act like walls in between the campsites, giving you privacy and your own personal cubby to camp in.

Charleston to Georgetown Area—Francis Marion National Forest

Campground	Total sites	Hookup sites	Max. RV length	Hookups	Toilets	Showers	Drinking water	Dump station	Recreation	Fee	Reservations
6 Buck Hall Campground	20	15	40'	E, W	Y	Y	Y	Y	H, M, R*, F, B, L, O*, P	$$–$$$	Y
7 Halfway Creek Trail Camp	*	0	n/a	N	N	N	N	N	H, M, R*, F*, B*, L*, O*	No Fee	N
8 Honey Hill Campground	7	0	n/a	N	V	N	N	N	H, M, R, F*, B*, L*, O	No Fee	N
9 Elmwood Primitive Campground	*	0	30'	N	V	N	Y	N	H, M, R, F*, B*, L*, O	No Fee	N

* See campground entry for specific information

6 Buck Hall Campground

Location: About 30 miles northeast of Charleston, and about 6 miles southwest of McClellanville
Season: Year-round
Sites: 20
Maximum length: 40 feet
Facilities: Flush toilets, hot showers, electric, water, fire rings, picnic tables, lantern holders, dump station, pet friendly
Fee per night: $$–$$$
Management: Francis Marion National Forest
Contact: (843) 336-3248; www.fs.usda.gov/recarea/scnfs/recreation/camping-cabins/recarea/?recid=47291&actid=29; for reservations, call (877) 444-6777 or visit www.recreation.gov
Finding the campground: From the junction of US 17 and SC 41 near Whitehall Terrace, drive north on US 17 for 19.8 miles to a right onto Buck Hall Landing Road (FR 242) and travel for 0.6 mile to the campground on your right.
    From the junction of US 17 and SC 45 in McClellanville, drive south on US 17 for approximately 6.2 miles to a right onto Buck Hall Landing Road (FR 242) and follow the directions above.
GPS coordinates: N33 02.426 / W79 33.775
Maps: *DeLorme: South Carolina Atlas and Gazetteer* page 56, F5
About the campground: Situated right alongside the Intracoastal Waterway, the Buck Hall campground and recreation area has an ideal location. Benches line the waterway, while a steady breeze helps keep the bugs away. The area is popular with boaters and anglers alike, and offers seafarers easy access to Bulls Bay and the Cape Romain National Wildlife Refuge. There's a boat launch and two floating docks on the premises. Or, for the land lovers who simply enjoy camping

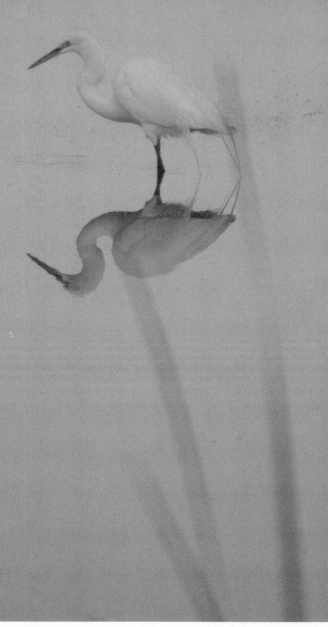

A white heron wades through the marsh.

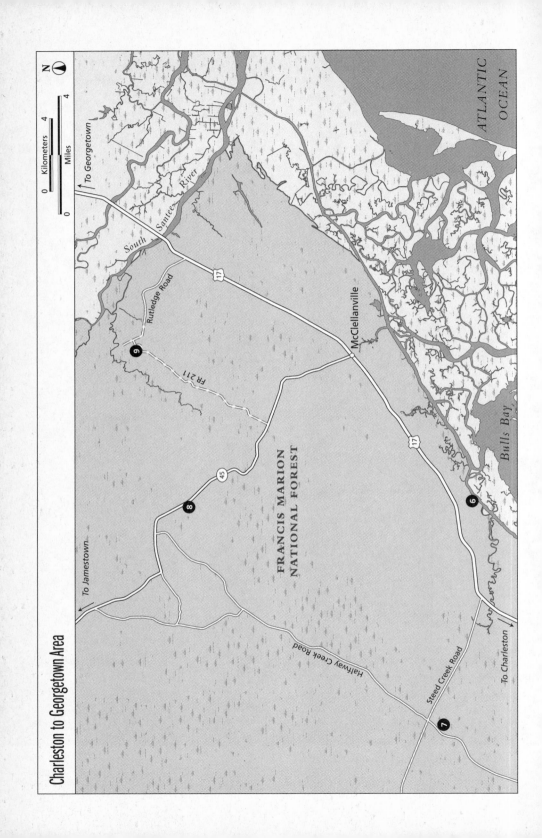

Charleston to Georgetown Area

N

0   Kilometers   4
0   Miles   4

To Georgetown

South Santee River

Rutledge Road

17

FR 211

9

45

8

To Jamestown

FRANCIS MARION NATIONAL FOREST

McClellanville

Halfway Creek Road

Steed Creek Road

7

To Charleston

17

6

Bulls Bay

ATLANTIC OCEAN

near the water, South Carolina's famous Palmetto Trail runs right through the property and is open to hikers and mountain bikers. With the main body of the Francis Marion National Forest just a few miles away, you also have easy access to miles of bridle and off-highway vehicle (OHV) trails. The campsites at Buck Hall are fairly open to one another, with a few trees placed here and there, so don't expect much privacy or shade for that matter. A handful of sites are dedicated for tent camping only.

7 Halfway Creek Trail Camp

Location: About 20 miles northeast of Charleston, and about 15 miles southwest of McClellanville
Season: Year-round
Sites: Open area, no set number of designated campsites
Maximum length: n/a
Facilities: Primitive fire rings, no water, no bathrooms, pet friendly
Fee per night: None
Management: Francis Marion National Forest
Contact: (843) 336-3248; www.fs.usda.gov/recarea/scnfs/recreation/camping-cabins/recarea/?recid=47301&actid=29
Finding the campground: From the junction of US 17 and NC 41 near Whitehall Terrace, drive north on US 17 for 16.5 miles to a left onto Steed Creek Road (SR 1032). Follow Steed Creek Road for 4.5 miles to a left onto Halfway Creek Road (SR 98). Travel for 0.5 mile to a left onto FR 5174 and follow it for less than 0.1 mile to where it dead-ends at the camping area.

From the junction of US 17 and NC 45 in McClellanville, drive south on US 17 for approximately 9.4 miles to a right onto Steed Creek Road (SR 1032) and follow the directions above.
GPS coordinates: N33 03.358 / W79 41.729
Maps: *DeLorme: South Carolina Atlas and Gazetteer* page 56, F4
About the campground: Often used by hunters and hikers alike, the Halfway Creek Trail Camp sits right along the Swamp Fox Trail. This 47-mile trail is part of South Carolina's famous Palmetto Trail, which traverses the entire state. The "swamp fox" was a moniker given to General Francis Marion during the Revolutionary War. The trail is open to hikers and mountain bikers, but be prepared to get your feet wet as you head out to explore the area, as a good portion of this trail cuts right through the Wambaw Swamp. If you prefer to travel via motor rather than self-propulsion, the Wambaw Cycle Trail is just a few miles up the road and is open for off-highway vehicle (OHV) use. Miles of bridle trails are also within easy reach and a quick jaunt down to the Buck Hall Recreation Area gives you plenty of opportunity to fish or launch a boat. There's a rifle range nearby as well, so don't be surprised if you hear gunfire in the distance. As for amenities, a primitive fire ring here and there is all you get; there's no bathroom, and the hand water pump hasn't worked in quite some time, so be sure you come prepared when you visit this rustic trail camp.

A fire tower stands tall at the entrance to Honey Hill Campground.

8 Honey Hill Campground

Location: About 33 miles northeast of Charleston, and about 8 miles northwest of McClellanville
Season: Year-round
Sites: 7
Maximum length: n/a
Facilities: Vault toilets, no water, fire rings, picnic tables, lantern holders, pet friendly
Fee per night: None
Management: Francis Marion National Forest
Contact: (843) 336-3248; www.fs.usda.gov/recarea/scnfs/recreation/camping-cabins/recarea/?recid=47299&actid=29
Finding the campground: From the junction of SC 45 and US 17 in McClellanville, drive north on SC 45 for 8.3 miles to the entrance to the campground on the left at FR 5012.
   From the junction of SC 45 and Alternate US 17 in Jamestown, drive south on SC 45 for approximately 12.0 miles to the entrance to the campground on the right.
GPS coordinates: N33 10.481 / W79 33.693
Maps: *DeLorme: South Carolina Atlas and Gazetteer* page 56, D5
About the campground: Crisp, clean, well-spaced, and well-groomed campsites greet you at this small, but wooded, campground. With a fire tower at its doorstep, Honey Hill is easily the nicest camping facility in the Francis Marion National Forest. Its location just minutes from the Wambaw Cycle Trail, the Jericho Horse Trail, and the Swamp Fox Trail makes it ideal to explore the forest by just about any means of travel. If you like the water, the Santee River is within easy reach. Or, if you prefer ocean access, head down to the coast to McClellanville or to the Buck Hall Recreation Area. Both have boat ramps that are open to the public and give you easy access to the Intracoastal Waterway or the Atlantic Ocean.

9 Elmwood Primitive Campground

Location: About 6 miles north of McClellanville, and about 17 miles southwest of Georgetown
Season: Year-round
Sites: Open field, no set number of designated campsites
Maximum length: 30 feet
Facilities: Vault toilets, hand water pump, primitive fire rings, pet friendly
Fee per night: None
Management: Francis Marion National Forest
Contact: (843) 336-3248; www.fs.usda.gov/recarea/scnfs/recreation/camping-cabins/recarea/?recid=47297&actid=29
Finding the campground: From the junction of US 17 and SC 45 in McClellanville, drive north on US 17 for 6.4 miles to a left onto Rutledge Road (SR 857). Travel for 3.7 miles to a left onto FR 211 (Mill Branch). Travel for 0.2 mile to the stop sign, turn right, and travel less than 0.1 mile to the primitive camp on your left.

Massive trees grace the Elmwood area.

From the junction of US 17 and the Santee River Bridge near North Santee, drive south on US 17 for approximately 1.0 mile to a right onto Rutledge Road (SR 957) and follow the directions above.

GPS coordinates: N33 11.959 / W79 28.159

Maps: *DeLorme: South Carolina Atlas and Gazetteer* page 57, C6

About the campground: This primitive campground is composed of a large, open grassy field. Beautiful, massive oak trees surround the area, but the layout and location of the fire rings don't offer campers very much privacy. Elmwood sees most of its traffic during the hunting seasons and may seem quite barren at other times. Primitive fire rings here and there and a pair of vault toilets are the extent of the amenities. A single hand water pump provides campers with water, but there are no showers. I recommend bringing bug spray, as this area tends to be buggy nearly any time of the day. The historic Hampton Plantation is just down the road, and although Elmwood sits near the northeastern edge of the Francis Marion National Forest, it's still within easy enough reach to the many recreational activities this forest has to offer. You can mountain bike on the South Tibwin Trail, or hop on horseback and head out on the Tuxbury or Jericho Trails. If you prefer fishing, or have a boat, head over to the Buck Hall Recreation Area and launch your vessel from there. But remember, if you do fish at either Buck Hall, in the Santee River, or anywhere within the national forest, you must have a South Carolina state fishing license in your possession.

Myrtle Beach Area

Campground	Total sites	Hookup sites	Max. RV length	Hookups	Toilets	Showers	Drinking water	Dump station	Recreation	Fee	Reservations
10 **Huntington Beach** **State Park**	143	133	85'	E, W, S*	F	Y	Y	Y	H, C, S, F, B*, L*, P	$$-$$$	Y
11 **Myrtle Beach State** **Park**	300	270	70'	E, W, S*	F	Y	Y	Y	H, M, R*, S, F, B*, HS, L*, P, **	$$$	Y

* See campground entry for specific information

10 Huntington Beach State Park

Location: 16148 Ocean Hwy., Murrells Inlet; about 20 miles northeast of Georgetown, and about 15 miles southwest of Myrtle Beach
Season: Year-round
Sites: 133; 6 primitive tent sites, 4 group campsites are also available and can accommodate up to 25 people
Maximum length: 85 feet
Facilities: Flush toilets, hot showers, electric, water, sewer, fire rings, picnic tables, dump station, ice and firewood for sale, pet friendly
Fee per night: $$-$$$
Management: South Carolina Department of Natural Resources
Contact: (843) 237-4440; www.southcarolinaparks.com/huntingtonbeach/camping.aspx; for reservations call (866) 345-7275 or visit www.reserveamerica.com
Finding the campground: From the junction of US 17 and SC 707 in Murrells Inlet, drive south on US 17 for 4.5 miles to the entrance to the park on your left.
   From the junction of US 17 and US 701 in Georgetown, drive north on US 17 for 18.0 miles to the entrance to the park on your right.
GPS coordinates: N33 30.783 / W79 04.311
Maps: *DeLorme: South Carolina Atlas and Gazetteer* page 50, F1
About the campground: With 3 miles of oceanfront property, a saltwater marsh, and a freshwater lagoon, Huntington Beach State Park breeds diversity. As pelicans fly overhead, you can see American alligators basking in the sun near the Mullet Pond. Make sure you bring your binoculars, since over three hundred species of birds have been known to inhabit the park, and sea turtles build their nests upon the shore. Needless to say, the park gives you beach access at both the north and south ends, and surprisingly, dogs are also welcome on the south end of the beach but must remain on a leash at all times. A 2-mile nature trail and a paved bike path allow you to explore the far reaches of the park. Take a dip in the ocean, or fish from the beach, but make sure you have a South Carolina state fishing license before casting your line. You are welcome to launch a kayak from the beach, but you must drag it down to the water. Or you can bring your canoe or kayak to Oyster Landing, just north of the park off US 17. But be forewarned, the water is tidal,

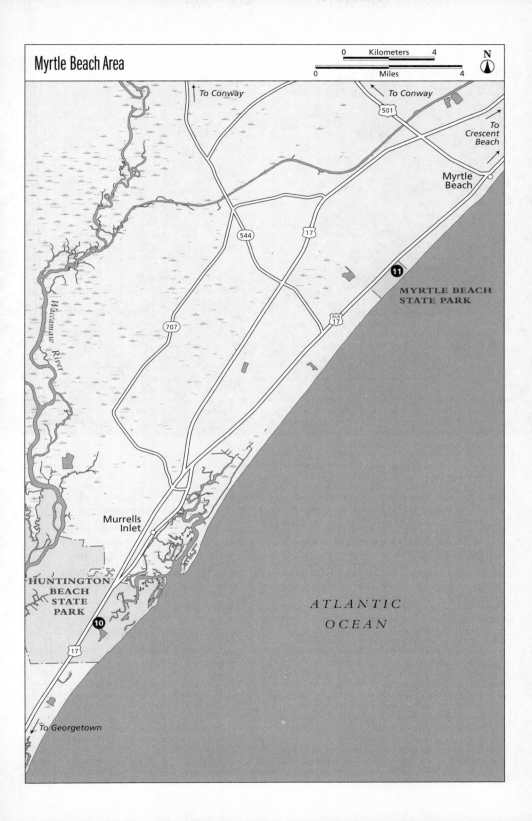

Myrtle Beach Area

Kilometers

Miles

N

To Conway

To Conway

501

To
Crescent
Beach

Myrtle
Beach

544

17

11

MYRTLE BEACH
STATE PARK

707

BUS
17

Waccamaw River

Murrells
Inlet

HUNTINGTON
BEACH
STATE
PARK

10

17

*ATLANTIC
OCEAN*

To Georgetown

Sunrise over the ocean is a highlight at Huntington Beach.

so be cautious where you park your vehicle, in case the tide comes in while you're out paddling. Huntington Beach has another unique feature: Atalaya. Atalaya was once home to Archer and Anne Hyatt Huntington and is now registered as a National Historic Landmark. You can tour the premises of this 1930s home, or even rent it out for weddings and special events. The park in general and the campground are well run and heavily used throughout the year. RVs fill up the majority of campsites, but don't be discouraged; even in the farthest loop, the sound of the ocean spills into your tent. In the still of the night, as the sun sets and the air moistens with dew, the sound of the ocean fills the air and washes the day away. You quickly forget you're in a crowded campground as the fire crackles and the waves crash upon the sand. Take a day trip to the neighboring Brookgreen Gardens to see a wide variety of both flora and fauna alike. And if you're a seafood lover, you're in luck! Just up the road in the quaint little town of Murrells Inlet there are seafood restaurants as far as the eye can see.

11 Myrtle Beach State Park

Location: 4401 S. Kings Hwy., Myrtle Beach; about 3 miles south of downtown Myrtle Beach
Season: Year-round
Sites: 270; 30 rustic tent sites in the overflow camping area; groups of up to 200 people are welcome to use the overflow camping area during the off season; cabin rentals are also available
Maximum length: 70 feet, but there are a limited number of sites that can accommodate this size RV
Facilities: Flush toilets, hot showers, electric, water, sewer, fire rings, picnic tables, dump station, laundry facility, ice and firewood for sale, pet friendly
Fee per night: $$$
Management: South Carolina Department of Natural Resources
Contact: (843) 238-5325; www.southcarolinaparks.com/myrtlebeach/camping.aspx; for reservations call (866) 345-7275 or visit www.reserveamerica.com
Finding the campground: From the junction of US 17 and US 501 in Myrtle Beach, drive south on US 17 for 3.7 miles to the entrance to the park on the left.

From the junction of US 17 Business and SC 544 in Surfside Beach, drive north on US 17 Business for 1.9 miles to the entrance to the park on the right.
GPS coordinates: N33 39.196 / W78 55.832
Maps: *DeLorme: South Carolina Atlas and Gazetteer* page 50, D3

A flock of pelicans flies overhead.

The picnic area at Myrtle Beach State Park is quite impressive.

About the campground: Tall trees and colorful wildflowers line the road as you enter Myrtle Beach State Park. It's touted as South Carolina's very first state park, and they've done a fabulous job of keeping up appearances since its inception in 1936. This beachfront park has a full mile of oceanfront property, and large picnic shelters line the grassy fields just west of the sand dunes. A fishing pier juts out into the Atlantic Ocean, and you can fish from the pier or the shore, as long as you have a South Carolina state fishing license. A small fee ($) is required to walk out onto the pier, and the pier store doubles as a tackle shop where they offer fishing reel rentals for an additional fee ($). During the winter months, visitors are welcome to bring their own horses and ride on the beach, but you must first obtain a permit from the park, again for an additional fee ($$$). Also, horse owners must show proof of a negative Coggins test, and horses are not allowed in the park overnight. Feel free to launch a kayak from the beach, but you must drag it down to the water first. Go for a dip in the ocean, or take a stroll alongside it. Simply sun yourself, or bring an umbrella and read a book. Either way, the shell-lined shore here, in what's known as the Grand Strand, is outstanding. Remarkably, the landscape is not just limited to the beach. The park is also home to a wonderful maritime forest, where oak trees flourish and fragrant magnolias blossom. A few trails pass through the forest and are open to hikers and mountain bikers. Birdlife abounds throughout the park, with over a hundred different species taking up residence within. Bring your binoculars, and keep a keen eye out. They have brightly colored cardinals and red-bellied woodpeckers, adorable chickadees and hummingbirds, and even the regal bald eagle can sometimes be seen soaring high above. A recreation area has a horseshoe pit, and you can even check out equipment to play games like bocce and cornhole. The campground is surprisingly wooded, especially since it sits just beside the beach. Some areas are more crowded than others, but with the sound of the waves lulling you to sleep at night, and the multitude of birds singing as you rise, Myrtle Beach State Park easily makes it on the Author's Favorites list. The town of Myrtle Beach is just up the road and reminds me of Orlando, Florida, or Gatlinburg, Tennessee. With tourist attractions galore, you will not be at a loss for things to do. From the whimsical Ripley's attractions, to several water parks, or perhaps you've dreamt of driving a real Nascar race car. Well, you can do it all in Myrtle Beach. There are several championship golf courses for the adults and putt-putt mini golf for the little ones. Whether you visit the Myrtle Beach boardwalk and watch the Ferris wheel shine in the night sky, or never leave the confines of the park, you will certainly enjoy this place.

Florence Area

Campground	Total sites	Hookup sites	Max. RV length	Hookups	Toilets	Showers	Drinking water	Dump station	Recreation	Fee	Reservations
12 **Lynches River County Park**	17	2	50'	E, W	F	Y	Y	N	H, M, S*, B*, L*, A, BB, P, **	$-$$	Y

* See campground entry for specific information

12 Lynches River County Park

Location: 5094 County Park Rd., Coward; about 7 miles south of Florence and about 12 miles north of Lake City
Season: Year-round; closed Thanksgiving, Christmas Eve, and Christmas Day
Sites: 17
Maximum length: 50 feet
Facilities: Flush toilets, hot showers, electric*, water, fire rings, picnic tables, trash cans, pet friendly
Fee per night: $-$$
Management: Florence County Parks and Recreation Commission
Contact: (843) 389-0550 or (843) 667-0920; www.lynchesriverpark.com/lrp.aspx
Finding the campground: From the junction of US 52 and US 301 in Effingham, drive south on US 52 for 1.3 miles to a right onto Old Highway Number 4 at the sign for Lynches River County Park. Travel for 1.8 miles to a right onto County Park Road (SR 1679). Follow this for 0.6 mile to the entrance to the park.

From the junction of SC 541 and SC 403 at Byrds Crossroads, drive east on SC 541/Old Highway Number 4 for 0.6 mile. Bear left here, continuing to follow Old Highway Number 4 for another 7.0 miles to a left onto County Park Road, and follow the directions above.
GPS coordinates: N34 02.033 / W79 47.266
Maps: *DeLorme: South Carolina Atlas and Gazetteer* page 39, E7
About the campground: This Florence County Park is quite interesting and quite popular with the locals. A ball field and the "Splash Pad" mini water park are definitely the highlights, as is the newly added archery range and, of course, the river itself. Lynches River runs right by the park, and a lovely canoe launch is open to the public, as are canoe and kayak rentals. The park's canoe landing sits nearly dead in the middle of the 111-mile Lynches River Scenic River Trail. So if you're a paddler, this is a fantastic place to explore. If you'd rather stay on dry land, a boardwalk leads you out along the water's edge, and a couple of hiking trails also allow you to peruse the park; mountain bikes are welcome on these trails as well. There's an Environmental Discovery Center (EDC) that offers all sorts of activities and programs throughout the year. The EDC also showcases several indigenous species such as turtles,

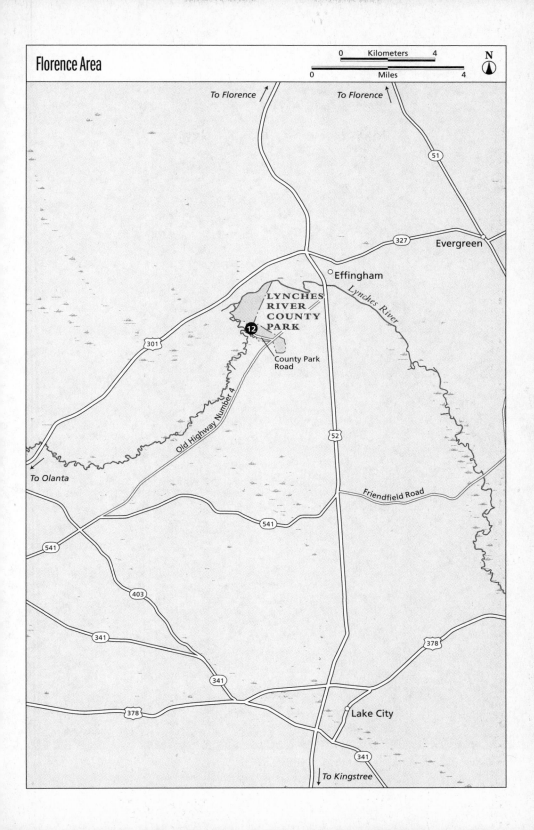

Florence Area

Kilometers 0 — 4
Miles 0 — 4

N

To Florence
To Florence

51

327
Evergreen

Effingham

LYNCHES RIVER COUNTY PARK

Lynches River

12

301

County Park Road

Old Highway Number 4

To Olanta

52

Friendfield Road

541

541

403

341

378

341

341

378

Lake City

341

To Kingstree

A wooden boardwalk leads out to view Lynches River.

frogs, toads, and an alligator. As for the campground, it's not near the river, so don't expect a waterfront view. Two campsites offer electric and water hookups. The remainder of the sites are not very well marked, but there's room for about fifteen other tent or pop-up campers; there are no hookups. As for the bathhouse, don't judge a book by its cover! What appears to be a double-wide vault toilet is actually a very nice bathhouse. Quite possibly the nicest campground bathroom in the state. The major drawback of this campground is that you can hear the neighborhood dogs barking throughout the night. That, coupled with the rumble of the train horn in the distance, and the occasional car passing by on US 52 can take away from the quiet. Aside from these distractions, Lynches River is a fairly peaceful park.

Dillon Area

Campground	Total sites	Hookup sites	Max. RV length	Hookups	Toilets	Showers	Drinking water	Dump station	Recreation	Fee	Reservations
13 **Little Pee Dee State Park**	51	32	40'	E, W	F	Y	Y	Y	H, M, B*, L*, P	$$–$$$	Y

* See campground entry for specific information

13 Little Pee Dee State Park

Location: 1298 State Park Rd., Dillon; about 8 miles southeast of Dillon, and about 8 miles north of Mullins
Season: Year-round
Sites: 50; 1 group camping area is also available that can accommodate up to 40 people
Maximum length: 40 feet, but there are a limited number of sites that can accommodate this size RV
Facilities: Flush toilets, hot showers, electric, water, fire rings, picnic tables, dump station, firewood for sale, pet friendly
Fee per night: $$–$$$
Management: South Carolina Department of Natural Resources
Contact: (843) 774-8872; www.southcarolinaparks.com/lpd/camping.aspx; for reservations call (866) 345-7275 or visit www.reserveamerica.com
Finding the campground: From the junction of SC 9 and SC 57 in Dillon, drive southeast on SC 9 for 5.9 miles to a right onto State Park Road (SR 22) and travel for 4.0 miles to the entrance to the park on your left.

From the junction of SC 57 and SC 41 in Fork, drive northwest on SC 57 for 2.3 miles to a right onto State Park Road (SR 22) at the sign for Little Pee Dee SP, and travel for 2.1 miles to the entrance to the park on your right.
GPS coordinates: N34 19.779 / W79 16.997
Maps: *DeLorme: South Carolina Atlas and Gazetteer* page 40, A4 & 31, H9
About the campground: Spanish moss hangs from the trees as you make your way through the park, en route to the campground. Resting along the banks of Lake Norton, some of the campsites literally sit right upon the shoreline, and the sites are surprisingly wooded, especially for waterfront camping. Named for the nearby Little Pee Dee River, this park is popular with locals and travelers alike, and you can clearly see why. They have hiking and mountain bike trails, boat rentals, and a place to launch your own nonmotorized boat in the lake. The lake is well stocked, so you can try your hand at fishing, as long as you have a South Carolina state fishing license prior to launching your line. There are playgrounds for the little ones and picnic shelters for the adults. Each campsite has its own water spigot, and many have electric as well. Off the beaten path, Little Pee Dee State Park offers a peaceful place to spend the night, or week for that matter, and is among my favorite

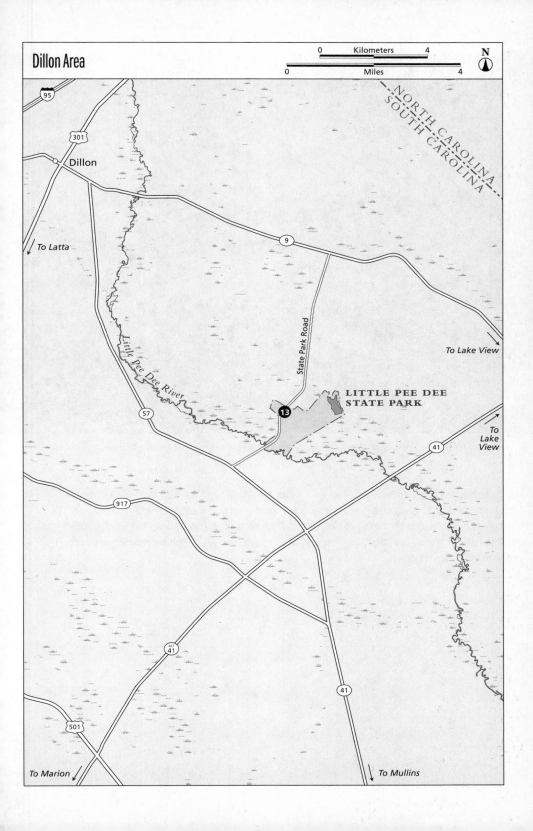

Dillon Area

0 Kilometers 4
0 Miles 4

N

95

301

Dillon

To Latta

NORTH CAROLINA
SOUTH CAROLINA

9

State Park Road

To Lake View

Little Pee Dee River

57

13 **LITTLE PEE DEE STATE PARK**

41

To Lake View

917

41

ALT 41

41

501

To Marion

To Mullins

A variety of boat rentals are available at Little Pee Dee State Park.

campgrounds in the state. If you're up for a quick excursion, head down to Mullins and visit the South Carolina Tobacco Museum. Or, if you have extra time, and a canoe, I highly recommend that you head out on the Little Pee Dee Scenic River Water Trail. This 27-mile river corridor flows through a picturesque floodplain forest and showcases the finest of South Carolina's natural environment in the region.

Midlands–Piedmont

Farmland sprawls across the middle portion of the state, painting the Piedmont like a tapestry, with the capital of Columbia sitting in the center. Wildflowers line the roadside, and horses come running up to greet you at the fence lines. Wisteria blossoms hang down from the trees, and their brilliant purple flowers decorate the countryside. The Savannah River borders the state to the west, and campsites await you right on the shores of Lakes Marion, J. Strom Thurmond, and Richard B. Russell. Stunning sunsets greet you as you sit in your camp chair and take in the view. You can cruise your boat right up to your site at many of the campgrounds within the region, or fish from your own backyard in your home away from home. Three of the four ranger districts of the Sumter National Forest can be found in the Midlands, and whether you ride on horseback, mountain bike, or off-highway vehicle (OHV), you're certain to find a trail that suits your needs. If you favor a simple hiking stick within your hand, almost every campground in the region has some sort of nature trail for you to get out and stretch your legs. From Ridgeland to Rock Hill, McCormick to Sumter, there's something for everyone. Go antiquing in Edgefield, or tour a gold mine site in McCormick. Visit the Rose Hill Plantation near Union, or see the floodplain forest of Congaree National Park. Wherever you choose, make yourself at home, and enjoy that small-town Southern appeal that the Midlands has to offer.

Vast farmland spans throughout the Midlands.

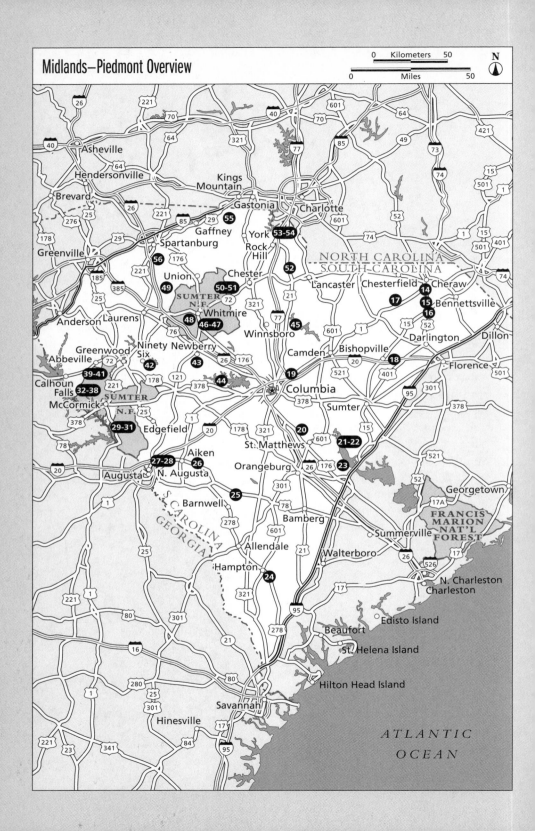

Kilometers
Miles

N

Asheville
Hendersonville
Brevard
Greenville

Kings
Mountain
Gastonia
Charlotte

Gaffney
Spartanburg

York
Rock
Hill

NORTH CAROLINA
SOUTH CAROLINA

Union
Chester

SUMTER
N.F.

Whitmire

Lancaster
Chesterfield
Cheraw
Bennettsville

Anderson
Laurens
Winnsboro

Darlington
Dillon

Greenwood
Ninety
Six
Newberry
Camden
Bishopville
Florence

Abbeville

Calhoun
Falls
McCormick

SUMTER
N.F.

Columbia
Sumter

Edgefield

Aiken
St. Matthews

Augusta
N. Augusta
Orangeburg

Barnwell

SOUTH
CAROLINA
GEORGIA

Bamberg

Georgetown

**FRANCIS
MARION
NAT'L
FOREST**

Allendale
Summerville

Hampton
Walterboro

N. Charleston
Charleston

Edisto Island

Beaufort
St. Helena Island

Hilton Head Island

Savannah
Hinesville

ATLANTIC

OCEAN

Bennettsville Area

Campground	Total sites	Hookup sites	Max. RV length	Hookups	Toilets	Showers	Drinking water	Dump station	Recreation	Fee	Reservations
14 **Cheraw State Park**	25	17	45'	E, W	F	Y	Y	Y	H, M, R, S, F, B*, L*, G, V, HS, P, **	$-$$	Y
15 **H. Cooper Black Jr. State Recreation Area**	38	27	None	E, W	F	Y	Y	Y	H, R, F*, P, **	$-$$	Y
16 **Lake Darpo County Park**	7	2	40'	E,W, S*	F	Y	Y	N	F, B, L, BB, V, T, P	$$	Y*

* See campground entry for specific information

14 Cheraw State Park

Location: 100 State Park Rd., Cheraw; about 4 miles south of Cheraw, and about 24 miles north of Darlington

Season: Year-round

Sites: 17; 5 equestrian/primitive tent sites, 2 group camp areas are also available and can accommodate up to 96 and 120 people each; 1 boat-in campsite is also available; cabin rentals are also available

Maximum length: 45 feet

Facilities: Flush toilets, hot showers, electric, water, fire rings, picnic tables, lantern holders, dump station, pet friendly

Fee per night: $-$$

Management: South Carolina Department of Natural Resources

Contact: (843) 537-9656; www.southcarolinaparks.com/cheraw/camping.aspx; for reservations call (866) 345-7275 or visit www.reserveamerica.com

Finding the campground: From the junction of US 52 and US 1 near Cheraw, drive south on US 52 for approximately 1.3 miles to the entrance to Cheraw State Park on your right. Note: You will pass the first entrance to the state park on your right. To get to the campground, take the second entrance.

From the junction of US 52 and US 15/US 401 in Society Hill, drive north on US 52 for 9.8 miles to the entrance to Cheraw State Park on your left.

GPS coordinates: N34 38.456 / W79 53.551

Maps: *DeLorme: South Carolina Atlas and Gazetteer* page 30, C1

About the campground: On one side of Lake Juniper sits the campground, on the other is the main body of the park. With a sand volleyball court, 18-hole golf course, playground, and picnic area right next to the lake, you're never at a loss for things to do. That, combined with camping options for just about everyone, puts Cheraw State Park on the Author's Favorites list. The family campground is intimate and made up of a single loop with a bathhouse in the

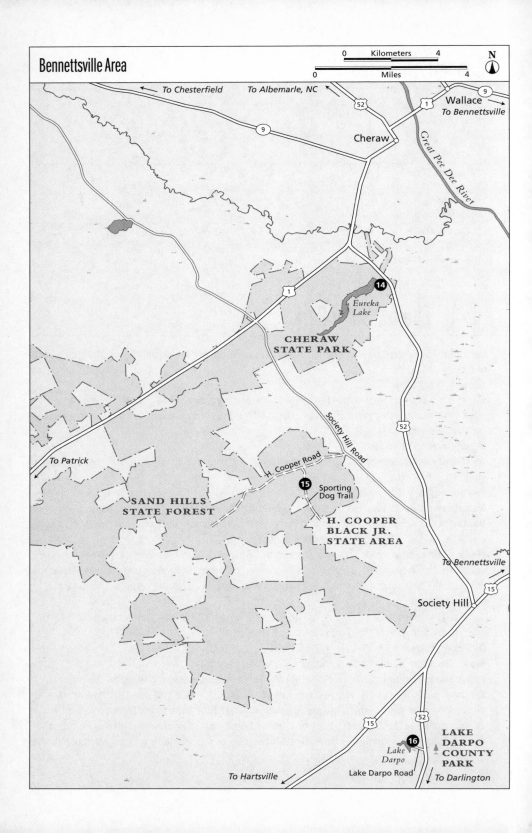

Bennettsville Area

To Chesterfield

To Albemarle, NC

Wallace

To Bennettsville

Cheraw

Great Pee Dee River

14

Eureka Lake

CHERAW STATE PARK

Society Hill Road

To Patrick

H. Cooper Road

15

Sporting Dog Trail

SAND HILLS STATE FOREST

H. COOPER BLACK JR. STATE AREA

To Bennettsville

Society Hill

16

Lake Darpo

LAKE DARPO COUNTY PARK

To Hartsville

Lake Darpo Road

To Darlington

Kilometers

Miles

N

Canoes and kayaks are ready for rental at Cheraw State Park.

middle. Many of the sites rest right upon the shores of Lake Juniper, and the lake is visible from every site in the campground. This waterfront location allows a slow but steady breeze to cast upon your campfire, lighting the embers within. The park also offers boat-in camping, equestrian camping, and a unique group camp opportunity with primitive cabins, and Lake Juniper still in view. The historic town of Cheraw is just minutes away, but with so much to do on the premises, you may not want to leave the park once you arrive. There are boat rentals available, a boat launch (limited to boats with less than 10 hp motors), a swimming area, and a fishing pier. If you prefer to explore the park by land, you can do so on foot, bike, or horseback. That's right: this park has hiking, mountain bike, and bridle trails. A wonderful loaner program allows you to borrow fishing poles, badminton, volleyball, horseshoes, and other equipment from the park office. But before you cast your line in the lake, be sure to have a South Carolina state fishing license also in hand.

15 H. Cooper Black Jr. State Recreation Area

Location: 279 Sporting Dog Trail, Cheraw; about 11 miles south of Cheraw, and about 19 miles north of Darlington
Season: Year-round
Sites: 38; backcountry camping is also available
Maximum length: None
Facilities: Flush toilets, hot showers, electric, water, fire rings, picnic tables, lantern holders, dump station, ice, firewood and horse shavings for sale, pet friendly
Fee per night: $-$$
Management: South Carolina Department of Natural Resources
Contact: (843) 378-1555; www.southcarolinaparks.com/hcb/camping.aspx; reservations for some sites must be made by contacting the park directly; other sites may be reserved by calling (866) 345-7275 or visiting www.reserveamerica.com
Finding the campground: From the junction of US 52 and US 15/US 401 in Society Hill, drive north on US 52 for 2.5 miles to a left onto Society Hill Road (SR 20) at the sign for H. Cooper Black Jr. Recreation Area, and travel for 2.9 miles to a left onto gravel H. Cooper Road. Follow H. Cooper Road for 1.3 miles to a left onto Sporting Dog Trail and the entrance to the recreation area.
GPS coordinates: N34 34.027 / W79 55.253
Maps: *DeLorme: South Carolina Atlas and Gazetteer* page 30, E1
About the campground: Rolling hills covered with long-leaf pine trees dot the countryside throughout the H. Cooper Black Jr. Recreation Area. Known as a premier equestrian destination, the rec. area has over 25 miles of bridle trails that crisscross the property, but that's just the tip of the iceberg. A barn with twenty-four stalls stands near the entrance to the property, and there's a show ring, a manure bin, plenty of parking for your horse trailer, and they even have a horse washing station. The park has three campground areas, known as the Barn loop, the Arena loop, and a primitive tent camping area. The Barn and Arena loops are outlined by corrals, and every campsite in these loops has a couple of corrals next to it. If you do bring a horse to camp with you overnight, you must either stable them in the barn, or keep them in a corral for an additional fee ($$). There are eleven primitive campsites, and they are the only place in the park that you can tether your horse to a tree overnight. I personally prefer the Arena loop over the Barn loop or primitive area, but quite honestly, not even this loop offers that much privacy. It does, however, seem to be a bit more shaded than the others. The recreation area hosts many events throughout the year, so you may want to check for availability prior to planning your trip. Not only is this horse country, but they also have three ponds and two open grassy fields. Believe it or not, you can actually rent a pond or a field for a whole day or a half. And surprisingly, they do rent out often. That's because H. Cooper Black Jr. is the biggest location in the South that plays host to many AKC retriever events and "hunt tests" for retriever dogs. It's even home to the Bird Dog Field Trial Regional Championships. Many competitors and breeders use this as a training facility to hone their dogs' abilities. If you've never seen these dogs in action, it's quite a sight to watch. A number of kennels are also available to rent for an additional fee ($), but the kennels are in a remote location, a good distance away from the campground. A single picnic shelter sits near the Wood Duck Pond, and all three ponds are stocked with fish. Visitors are welcome to fish from the banks, as long as the pond is not rented for the day, and provided that you have your South Carolina state fishing license. The bridle trails are open to hikers as well, but you may want to watch your step as you explore this 7,000-acre piece of horse heaven.

An odd-looking silo sits near the roadside on the way to H. Cooper Black State Recreation Area.

16 Lake Darpo County Park

Location: 100 Lake Rd., Society Hill; about 7 miles south of Cheraw and about 7 miles west of Bennettsville
Season: Year-round
Sites: 7
Maximum length: 40 feet
Facilities: Flush toilets, hot showers, electric, water, charcoal grill, picnic tables, trash cans, pet friendly
Fee per night: $$
Management: Darlington County Parks and Recreation Commission
Contact: (843) 398-4700; www.darlingtoncounty.org/stay_details.php?Lake-Darpo-27
Finding the campground: From the junction of US 52/US 401 and US 15 near Society Hill, drive south on US 52/US 401 for 2.2 miles to a right onto Lake Darpo Road (SR785) at the sign for Lake Darpo. Travel for 0.3 mile to the entrance to the park at the end of the road.

From the junction of US 52 and SC 34 in Darlington, drive north on US 52 for approximately 11.8 miles to a left onto Lake Darpo Road and follow the directions above.
GPS coordinates: N34 27.504 / W79 52.820
Maps: *DeLorme: South Carolina Atlas and Gazetteer* page 30, D2
About the campground: This tiny county park makes you feel like you've stepped back in time. Two RV campsites and a handful of primitive tent sites comprise the camping at Lake Darpo. The RV sites sit directly across from each other, and one has electric, water, and sewer hookups, while the other just has electric and water. As for the tent sites, there are no designated sites, simply a flat area, amid the trees, to pitch your tent. The lake itself is clearly the highlight here, with a small fishing pier and an unpaved boat ramp. While the park does offer several other activities, they are in need of some TLC. There's a basketball court, tennis court, and volleyball net, not to mention the old-time playground that seems to have come straight from my youth. The campsites are lacking privacy, but since this park is tiny and off the beaten path, and reservations are required, you may just have the whole place to yourself.

Old-time playground ponies sit alongside Lake Darpo.

Chesterfield Area

Campground	Total sites	Hookup sites	Max. RV length	Hookups	Toilets	Showers	Drinking water	Dump station	Recreation	Fee	Reservations
17a Sand Hills State Forest–Sugarloaf Mountain Family Campground	7	0	40'	N	V	N	N	N	H, R*, M*, F, B, L, P	$$	Y*
17b Sand Hills State Forest–Sugarloaf Mountain Equine Campground	8	0	40'	N	V	N	N	N	H, R*, M*, F, B, L, P	$$	Y*

* See campground entry for specific information

17 Sand Hills State Forest–Sugarloaf Mountain Family and Equine Campgrounds

Location: Within Sand Hills State Forest; about 12 miles south of Chesterfield and about 9 miles west of Patrick
Season: Year-round
Sites: 15
Maximum length: 40 feet
Facilities: Vault toilet, fire rings, picnic tables, trash cans, pet friendly
Fee per night: $$
Management: South Carolina Forestry Commission
Contact: (843) 498-6478; www.state.sc.us/forest/refshill.htm
Finding the campground: Sites 1–7: From the junction of SC 145 and SC 109 at Campbell Crossroads, drive southeast on Hartsville-Ruby Road (SR 29, across from SC 109) for 4.6 miles to a left onto Scotch Road (FR 63) at the sign for Sand Hills State Forest Sugarloaf Mountain. Follow Scotch Road for 0.4 mile to a right onto Mountain Road and travel for 0.5 mile to campsites 1–7.

From the junction of US 1 and SC 102 in Patrick, drive south on US 1 for 5.1 miles to a right onto Hartsville-Ruby Road (SR 29) and travel for 2.9 miles to Scotch Road (FR 63). Turn right onto Scotch Road, and follow the directions above.

From the junction of US 1 and SC 145 in McBee, drive north on US 1 for 7.8 miles to a left onto Hartsville-Ruby Road and follow the directions above.

Finding the campground: Sites 8–15: From the junction of SC 145 and SC 109 at Campbell Crossroads, drive south on Hartsville-Ruby Road (SR 29, across from SC 109) for just over 4.6 miles to a left onto Gas Line Road. Follow Gas Line Road for 0.6 mile to campsites 8–15 on your left.

From the junction of US 1 and SC 102 in Patrick, drive south on US 1 for 5.1 miles to a right onto Hartsville-Ruby Road (SR 29) and travel for 2.9 miles to Gas Line Road at the sign for Sugarloaf Mountain Recreation Area. Turn right onto Gas Line Road, and follow the directions above.

Chesterfield Area

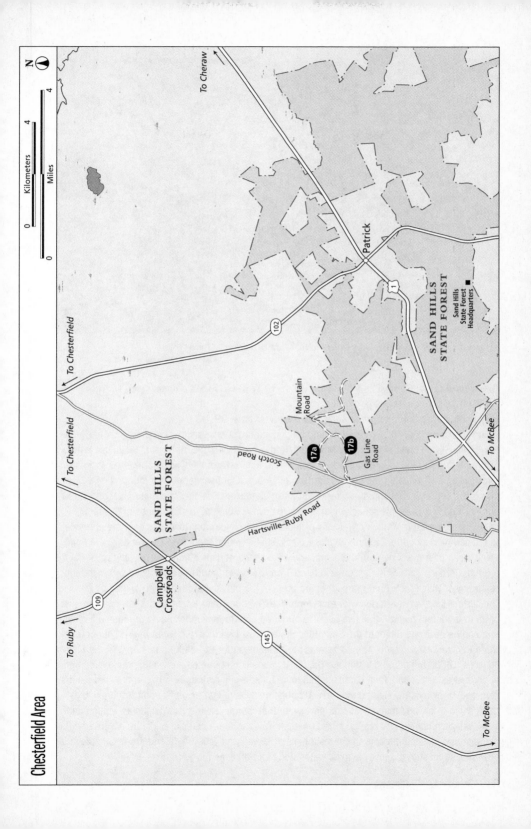

A wonderful picnic shelter overlooks the lake at Sugarloaf Mountain

GPS coordinates: Campsites #1–7: N34 35.493 / W80 07.718; Campsites #8–15: N34 34.942 / W80 07.634

Maps: *DeLorme: South Carolina Atlas and Gazetteer* page 29, D8

About the campground: Two separate and unique campgrounds greet you in the center of the Sand Hills State Forest at Sugarloaf Mountain. Known locally as "the mountain," Sugarloaf is actually more of a rise than a mountain. It hails about a hundred feet high, rising above the surrounding forest. Sites 1–7 make up the family campground. A beautiful fishing pond surrounded by rolling hills is the center attraction as you approach these campsites. The sites are quite large and spread out over nearly a mile, giving each camper ample privacy. Some of the campsites in this family camping area even have their own lovely picnic shelter. A single vault toilet sits near the entrance to the campground, and a wonderful stone picnic shelter with a fireplace in it overlooks the pond. Visitors can cast their line from the shore, or try their hand at fishing from the pier, but must have a South Carolina state fishing license in hand. Nearly a dozen ponds can be found within the forest, many of which have boat ramps that are open to the public, but there is no swimming allowed. The surrounding forest is laden with trails for hiking and horseback riding, and a few trails are also open to mountain bikes. A trail use permit is required prior to horseback riding or mountain biking, and can be obtained either at the Sand Hills State Forest Headquarters, or at the H. Cooper Black State Recreation Area barn. Annual permits are available at forest headquarters only. No off-highway vehicles (OHVs) are allowed within the Sand Hills State Forest. The equine campground is composed of campsites 8–15, and each campsite has room for several horse trailers. This entire area seems as though they recently cleared the land. Although many long-leaf pine trees still stand tall, they don't seem to provide much shade, or privacy for that matter, leaving your neighbors within plain view. Well-built horse stalls can be found on each site, and many miles of bridle trails surround the campground, making it a convenient resting place for you and your furry friend. No water spigots are provided, so be sure to bring plenty of water along for both you and your horse.

Bishopville Area

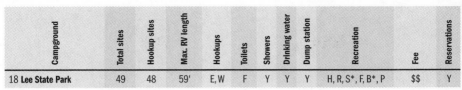

Campground	Total sites	Hookup sites	Max. RV length	Hookups	Toilets	Showers	Drinking water	Dump station	Recreation	Fee	Reservations
18 Lee State Park	49	48	59'	E, W	F	Y	Y	Y	H, R, S*, F, B*, P	$$	Y

* See campground entry for specific information

18 Lee State Park

Location: 487 Loop Rd., Bishopville; about 5 miles southeast of Bishopville, and about 21 miles west of Florence
Season: Year-round
Sites: 25 family; 23 equestrian; 1 group camping area is also available and can accommodate up to 100 people
Maximum length: 59 feet
Facilities: Flush toilets, hot showers, electric, water, fire rings, picnic tables, dump station, firewood for sale, pet friendly
Fee per night: $$
Management: South Carolina Department of Natural Resources
Contact: (803) 428-5307; www.southcarolinaparks.com/lee/camping.aspx; for reservations call (866) 345-7275 or visit www.reserveamerica.com
Finding the campground: From I-20 get off at exit 123 and drive north on Lee State Park Road (SR 22) for approximately 1.0 mile to the entrance to the park on the left.
   From the junction of US 15 and SC 341 in Bishopville, drive north/east on US 15 for approximately 2.4 miles to a right onto Lee State Park Road (SR 22) and travel for approximately 3.6 miles to the entrance to the park on the right.
GPS coordinates: N34 11.808 / W80 11.160
Maps: *DeLorme: South Carolina Atlas and Gazetteer* page 38, C3
About the campground: Stone pillars greet you at the entrance to this lovely state park. A mix of oak and pine trees scattered throughout the campground provide lots of shade, but the campsites could be spread out a little better. There are two distinct loops: one is your typical family-style campground, and the other is dedicated to equestrian campers. If you weren't told this, you wouldn't really be able to tell, except that the sites are a bit larger to accommodate horse trailers. Also, the horse camp has an area with several stalls to house your mount. The stalls are in a separate area, all lined up in a row, and not actually next to your campsite. Several miles of bridle trails run throughout the park, making this a ride-in/ride-out locale. If riding's not your thing, you can hike the horse trails or amble along the nature trail. Lynches River skirts the western border of the park, and you can fish from the

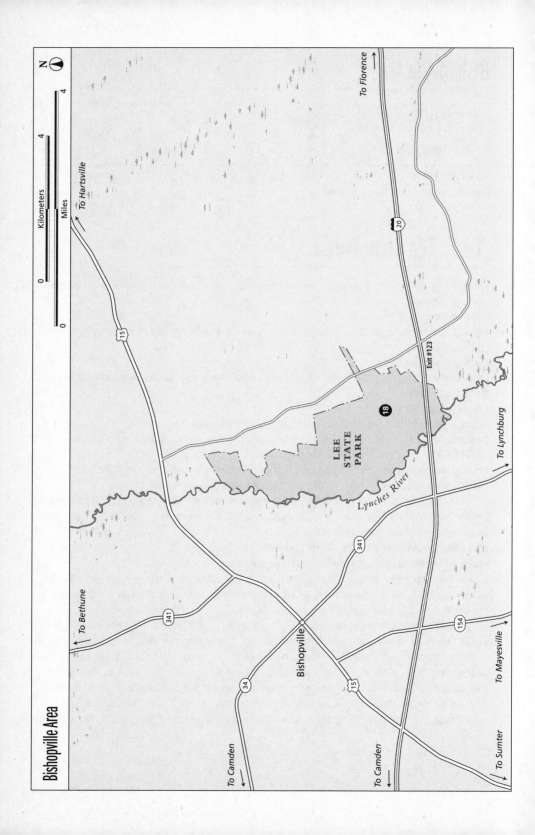

Bishopville Area

Rhododendron flowers adorn the entrance to Lee State Park.

banks within the park as long as you have a South Carolina state fishing license with you. You can launch a canoe or kayak from inside the park, or head up the road about 4 miles to one of several river access points. At the south end of the park is a lovely pond, which is open for swimming seasonally. Lee State Park offers several programs and activities year-round; for more information check out their website.

Columbia Area

	Campground	Total sites	Hookup sites	Max. RV length	Hookups	Toilets	Showers	Drinking water	Dump station	Recreation	Fee	Reservations
19	**Sesquicentennial State Park**	89	84	50'	E, W	F	Y	Y	Y	H, M, F, B*, V, HS, P, **, Dog Park	$$$	Y
20	**Congaree National Park–Longleaf Campground**	14	10	n/a	N	V	N	N	N	H, F, B*, L*, P	No Fee*	N

* See campground entry for specific information

19 Sesquicentennial State Park

Location: 9564 Two Notch Rd., Columbia; about 2 miles northeast of Columbia
Season: Year-round
Sites: 84; 5 primitive group camp areas are also available and can accommodate up to 25 people
Maximum length: 70 feet
Facilities: Flush toilets, hot showers, electric, water, fire rings, picnic tables, dump station, ice and firewood for sale, pet friendly
Fee per night: $$$
Management: South Carolina Department of Natural Resources
Contact: (803) 788-2706; www.southcarolinaparks.com/sesqui/camping.aspx; for reservations call (866) 345-7275 or visit www.reserveamerica.com
Finding the campground: From I-77 in Columbia, get off at exit 17 and follow US 1 north for 2.3 miles to the entrance to the park on the right.
GPS coordinates: N34 06.100 / W80 54.659
Maps: *DeLorme: South Carolina Atlas and Gazetteer* page 36, E4
About the campground: Sitting in the heart of the state, in the capital of Columbia, you will find Sesquicentennial State Park, known locally as "Sesqui." The campground is made up of two wooded loops, although the sites are a bit close together for such a wooded area. One loop is open seasonally, while the other remains open year-round. The park is easy to access given its location, but unfortunately, that same ease of access causes you to hear the constant hum of traffic throughout the day and night. The park is packed with many activities. Trails loop around a centrally located lake and are open to hiking and mountain biking. There's a softball field, sand volleyball court, and horseshoe pit on the premises. A boathouse sits near the lake, and you can rent out canoes, kayaks, john boats, and paddle boats seasonally. There is no boat ramp on the property, but you can bring your own boat and carry it to the water's edge for launching. Personal boats are limited to canoes and kayaks, or boats with electric trolling

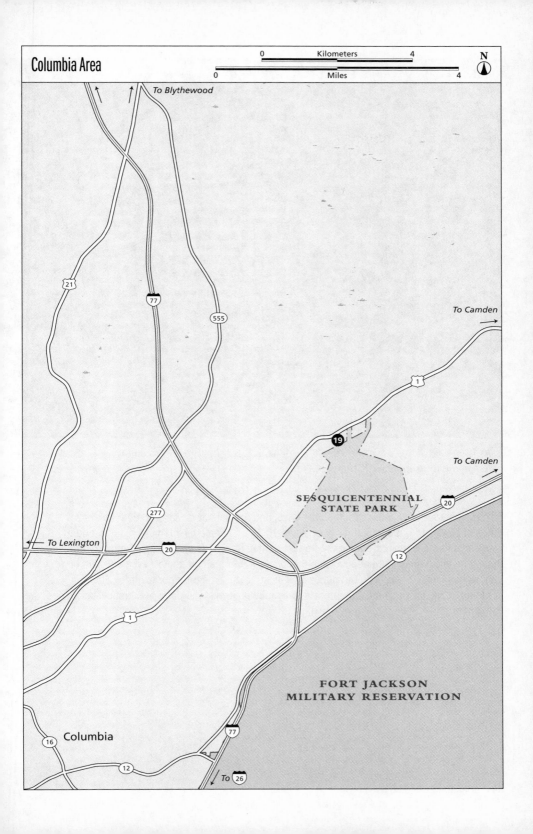

Columbia Area

To Blythewood

To Camden

To Camden

SESQUICENTENNIAL
STATE PARK

To Lexington

FORT JACKSON
MILITARY RESERVATION

Columbia

To

The historic log house at Sesquicentennial State Park was built in 1756, and is said to be the oldest standing structure in Richland County.

motors. There are playgrounds for the little ones, and the park has a large Retreat Center that can be rented out during the day or overnight. Often people host family reunions, bridal showers, and many other events at the Retreat Center. Since it is just minutes from downtown Columbia, this park is quite popular with the locals. To top it all off, there's even a 2-acre dog park within Sesqui State Park. But pet owners must obtain a permit prior to letting Fido run free in the dog park. Your pup must be present to acquire a permit, and proof of current vaccinations is required.

20 Congaree National Park–Longleaf Campground

Location: About 20 miles southeast of Columbia
Season: Year-round
Sites: 10; 4 group camp areas are also available and can accommodate up to 24 people each; backcountry camping is also available at the Bluff Campground
Maximum length: n/a
Facilities: Vault toilets, no water, fire rings, picnic tables, pet friendly
Fee per night: None, but you must register and obtain a free camping permit in person prior to camping
Management: National Park Service–Congaree National Park
Contact: (803) 776-4396; www.nps.gov/cong/planyourvisit/camping.htm
Finding the campground: From I-77 in Columbia, get off at exit 5 and drive east on SC 48 for 8.4 miles to a right onto Old Bluff Road (SR 734). Follow Old Bluff Road for 4.3 miles to the entrance to the park on your right. Follow the park road for 0.5 mile to the Longleaf Campground parking area on the left.

From the junction of SC 48 and SC 769 in Gadsden, drive west on SC 48 for 1.1 miles to a left onto Cedar Creek Road. Travel for 0.1 mile to a right onto Old Bluff Road (SR 734). Follow Old Bluff Road for 2.6 miles to the entrance to the park on your left. Follow the park road for 0.5 mile to the Longleaf Campground parking area on the left.
GPS coordinates: N33 50.135 / W80 49.692
Maps: *DeLorme: South Carolina Atlas and Gazetteer* page 45, A10 & 36, H5
About the campground: A short walk of less than 0.1 mile and up to 0.5 mile leads to the primitive campsites at Congaree National Park. Well-spaced and wooded, these staggered sites offer lots of privacy, and birds serenade you throughout the day. Famous for its biodiversity and champion trees, the park can be explored by foot or by canoe or kayak. Tall trees tower overhead, humbling you as you pass through the park, in awe of the nature around you. Over 25 miles of hiking trails and a 2.5-mile boardwalk tread through the floodplain forest. Canoe and kayak launches can be found at all ends of the park, giving you several options to paddle on either Cedar Creek or the Congaree River. Fishing is a popular pastime here as well, but you must obtain a South Carolina state fishing license first, and fishing is prohibited in Weston Lake. With all this water surrounding you, the area does tend to get buggy, especially at dusk and dawn, so you may want to bring some citronella candles or some bug spray along. For an even more rustic experience, backcountry camping is also available at the Bluff Campground, and requires a 1.5-mile hike to get to. There is no fee to camp at either campground, but you must obtain a camping permit before spending the night. You can get a permit at the self-registration kiosk in the parking lot for the Longleaf Campground. Camping is on a first come-first served basis. The National Park Service asks that you do not bring firewood into the park, as this may introduce invasive species. Feel free to forage for felled wood to use in your campfire, but please do not cut any live trees or plants to burn.

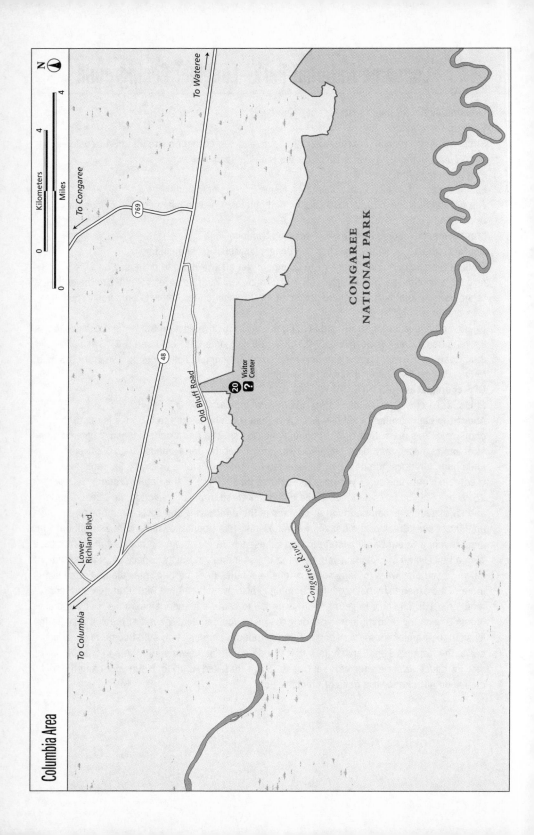

Columbia Area

N

0   4
Kilometers

0   4
Miles

To Columbia

To Wateree

To Congaree

769

48

Lower
Richland Blvd.

Old Bluff Road

Visitor
Center

20

?

Congaree River

CONGAREE
NATIONAL PARK

Manning Area

Campground	Total sites	Hookup sites	Max. RV length	Hookups	Toilets	Showers	Drinking water	Dump station	Recreation	Fee	Reservations
21 **Poinsett State Park**	55	25	53'	E, W	F	Y	Y	Y	H, M, S, F, B*, L*, R*, O*, P	$$	Y
22 **Mill Creek County Park**	120	120	None	E, W	F	Y	Y	Y	H, M, R, F, B*, O*, P	$-$$	Y
23a **Santee State Park: Cypress View Campground**	47	47	40'	E, W	F	Y	Y	Y	H, M, S, F, B, L, T, P	$$	Y
23b **Santee State Park: Lakeshore Campground**	116	111	40'	E, W	F	Y	Y	Y	H, M, S, F, B, L, T, P	$$	Y

* See campground entry for specific information

21 Poinsett State Park

Location: 6660 Poinsett Park Rd., Wedgefield; about 20 miles northwest of Manning, and about 13 miles southwest of Sumter
Season: Year-round
Sites: 50; 5 group camp areas are also available and can accommodate up to 50 people each; cabin rentals are also available
Maximum length: 55 feet, but there are a limited number of sites that can accommodate this size RV
Facilities: Flush toilets, hot showers, electric, water, fire rings, picnic tables, dump station, firewood for sale, pet friendly
Fee per night: $$
Management: South Carolina Department of Natural Resources
Contact: (803) 494-8177; www.southcarolinaparks.com/poinsett/camping.aspx; for reservations call (866) 345-7275 or visit www.reserveamerica.com
Finding the campground: From the junction of SC 261 and SC 120 in Pinewood, drive north on SC 261 for 5.9 miles to a left onto Poinsett Park Road (SR 63) at the sign for Poinsett State Park, and travel for 1.7 miles to the entrance to the park.

From the junction of SC 261 and SC 763 in Wedgefield, drive south on SC 261 for 6.1 miles to a right onto Poinsett Park Road and follow the directions above.
GPS coordinates: N33 48.050 / W80 32.003
Maps: *DeLorme: South Carolina Atlas and Gazetteer* page 46, A3
About the campground: Rolling hill topography greets you as you travel through Poinsett State Park, and the means of travel is entirely up to you. The park has trails for hiking and mountain biking, and the property butts up to the Manchester State Forest, where you can extend your hike or bike. The neighboring state forest also has miles of bridle and off-highway vehicle (OHV) trails

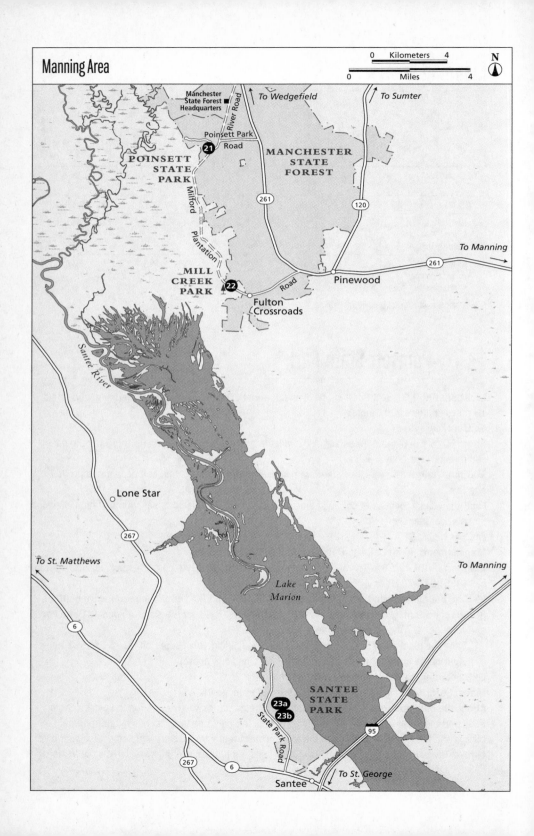

Manning Area

0 Kilometers 4
0 Miles 4

N

Manchester
State Forest
Headquarters

To Wedgefield

To Sumter

Poinsett Park
Road

21

River Road

**POINSETT
STATE
PARK**

**MANCHESTER
STATE
FOREST**

261

120

Milford

Plantation

To Manning

261

**MILL
CREEK
PARK**

22

Road

Pinewood

Fulton
Crossroads

Santee River

Lone Star

To St. Matthews

267

Lake
Marion

To Manning

6

**SANTEE
STATE
PARK**

State Park Road

23a
23b

95

267

6

To St. George

Santee

A small waterfall sits near the site of an old mill at Poinsett State Park.

open to the public, but you must obtain a permit before taking to the trail on horseback, bike, or OHV. A wide variety of tree species can be found throughout the park, and birdlife is abundant. As peaceful as Poinsett State Park seems when you arrive, don't be surprised if you hear the occasional rumble of an aircraft whizzing by. Several Air Force bases are located nearby, and there's a pistol range close by as well. A small lake sits near the "tea room," which doubles as the park office. This historic building was built by the Civilian Conservation Corps and is available to rent for special events. A spillway was also built by the CCC in the 1930s, and forms a pleasant man-made waterfall sitting near the site of the ruins where a gristmill once stood. You can fish in the pond, or take a dip at your own risk, but you must have a South Carolina state fishing license before you break out the rod and reel. Boat rentals are available, or you can bring your own boat, but you must carry it down to the lake, and personal boats are limited to less than 13 feet, and no gas-powered motors are allowed. If it's wide-open water you seek, take a trip down to Santee State Park, located on the western shores of Lake Marion.

22 Mill Creek County Park

Location: About 17 miles west of Manning and about 19 miles southwest of Sumter
Season: Year-round
Sites: 120; 1 group camp area is also available and can accommodate up to 150 people
Maximum length: None
Facilities: Flush toilets, hot showers, electric, water, picnic tables, dump station, pet friendly.
Fee per night: $-$$
Management: Sumter County Parks and Recreation
Contact: (803) 436-2248 or (803) 983-8350; www.sumtercountysc.org/?q=department/recreation/article/mill-creek-park
Finding the campground: From the junction of SC 261 and SC 120 in Pinewood, drive north on SC 261 for 1.0 mile to a left onto unmarked Milford Plantation Road (SR 808) at the sign for Mill Creek Park. Travel for 1.9 miles to a stop sign and continue straight across the intersection for another 0.8 mile to the entrance to the park on your right.

From the junction of SC 261 and SC 763 in Wedgefield, drive south on SC 261 for approximately 11.1 miles to a right onto Poinsett Park Road and follow the directions above.
GPS coordinates: N33 43.979 / W80 31.442
Maps: *DeLorme: South Carolina Atlas and Gazetteer* page 46, B4
About the campground: Rolling grassy fields greet you as you pass through the park and head toward the campground. But once you arrive, the flat, wide-open spread is more like a parking lot and does not offer much in the way of privacy, or shade for that matter. Popular with the local equine community, some of the sites have posts to tether your horse to, and Mill Creek Park is surrounded by miles and miles of bridle trails, which are also open to hikers. The campground also has stables to house your horse, and the stalls certainly get a lot more shade than the campsites do. The park hosts two big events annually in March and October, so you may want to check for availability before you visit during those months. A small pond graces the property with a fishing pier and a place to launch a canoe or kayak. Or, if you want to venture out farther and explore the Santee River, head down the road to Pack's Landing. You can launch your own canoe or kayak at the landing, or take a guided tour. There are plenty of outdoor opportunities for hiking, mountain biking, and off-highway vehicles (OHVs)in the neighboring Manchester State Forest. But, quite honestly, if you're not on horseback, I'd head up the road a few miles and camp at Poinsett State Park.

23 Santee State Park-Cypress View and Lakeshore Campgrounds

Location: 251 State Park Rd., Santee; about 20 miles southwest of Manning, and about 25 miles northeast of St. George
Season: Cypress View Campground: open year-round; Lakeshore Campground: March 1–end of November
Sites: Cypress View Campground: 47; Lakeshore Campground: 111; 5 primitive group camping areas are also available and can accommodate up to 20 people each; cabin rentals are also available
Maximum length: 40 feet
Facilities: Flush toilets, hot showers, electric, water, fire rings, picnic tables, dump station, ice and firewood for sale, laundry facilities, pet friendly
Fee per night: $$
Management: South Carolina Department of Natural Resources

An old draft horse is ready for an afternoon siesta.

Contact: (803) 854-2408; www.southcarolinaparks.com/santee/camping.aspx; for reservations call (866) 345-7275 or visit www.reserveamerica.com

Finding the campground: From I-95 get off at exit 98 and drive west on SC 6. Follow SC 6 for 1.1 miles to a right onto State Park Road (SR 105) at the sign for Santee State Park. Travel for 2.3 miles to a stop sign. Continue straight across for another 2.0 miles to the park Visitor's Center.

From the junction of SC 6 and SC 267 near Elloree, drive east on SC 6 for approximately 3.6 miles to a left onto State Park Road (SR 105) and follow the directions above.

GPS coordinates: Cypress Campground: N33 33.014 / W80 30.004; Lakeshore Campground: N33 30.719 / W80 28.568

Maps: *DeLorme: South Carolina Atlas and Gazetteer* page 46, F4

About the campground: On the eastern edge of the Piedmont, within easy reach of I-95 and resting along the western shores of Lake Marion, you will find Santee State Park. Two distinct campgrounds can be found within the park, the Cypress View and the Lakeshore. Several sites sit just above the banks of Lake Marion in both campgrounds, and the sites on the outside of the loops tend to have more privacy than those on the inside of the loops. I prefer the Lakeshore Campground over the Cypress View, primarily because it's remotely located from the main body of the park, and it's less than half the size of the Cypress View. Nearly every site at Lakeshore is shaded from the sun, and the sites are wonderfully spread out for the most part. Tents and RVs alike can enjoy the soft breeze that the waterfront sites at this isolated area have to offer. Alligators and sinkholes can be found along the trails near this portion of the park, and the steady sound of the birds singing in the background lulls you, blending in, much like white noise. A 7.5-mile mountain bike/hiking trail runs near the shoreline and connects the east and west portions of the park together. A few other trails can also be found within the park, but they are dedicated for hiking only. Lake Marion is obviously the climax at Santee State Park, but wildlife viewing, bird watching, sinkholes, tennis, playgrounds, and picnic shelters will also keep you entertained. Once a year, in late April, the town of Santee hosts the Santee Birding and Nature Festival. If you're a nature lover, this is a great off-site excursion. Or if you merely want to unwind—just relax a bit, sit a spell, lie in a hammock, and simply watch the water as it passes you by. If you are a water baby, you're in for a treat: swimming is permitted at your own risk. The park has two boat ramps, one near each campground. So you can launch your craft and spend an entire day exploring South Carolina's largest lake. That's right, at 110,000 acres, Lake Marion is the largest lake in the state. The park store doubles as a tackle shop, and you can fish from the banks, boat, or the park's wheelchair-accessible pier, provided you have a South Carolina state fishing license. For a special treat, you can take a guided tour on a pontoon boat and explore the upper reaches of Lake Marion and into the swampland of the Santee River. For more information on boat tours or to make a reservation, contact Fisheagle Tours directly at (800) 967-7739 or visit their website at www.fisheagle.net.

Hampton Area

Campground	Total sites	Hookup sites	Max. RV length	Hookups	Toilets	Showers	Drinking water	Dump station	Recreation	Fee	Reservations
24 **Lake Warren State Park: Group Camp**	1	0	n/a	N	F	N	Y	N	H, F, B, L, P	$$-$$$	Y*

* See campground entry for specific information

24 Lake Warren State Park: Group Camp

Location: 1079 Lake Warren Rd., Hampton; about 5 miles southwest of Hampton
Season: Year-round
Sites: 1 group site that can accommodate up to 50 people
Maximum length: n/a

The serenity of Lake Warren is astounding.

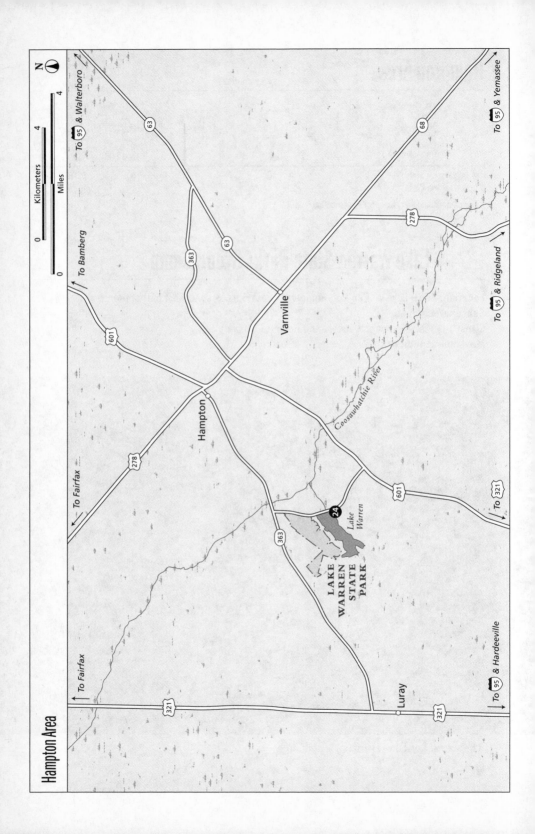

Hampton Area

Facilities: Flush toilets (in day-use area), water spigot, fire rings, picnic tables, pet friendly
Fee per night: $$–$$$
Management: South Carolina Department of Natural Resources
Contact: (803) 943-5051; www.southcarolinaparks.com/lakewarren/introduction.aspx
Finding the campground: From the junction of US 601 and US 278 in Hampton, drive south on US 601 for 3.7 miles to a right onto Lake Warren Road (SR 510) at the sign for Lake Warren SP. Travel for 1.1 miles to the entrance to the park on the left.

From the junction of SC 363 and US 321 in Luray, drive northeast on SC 363 for 3.1 miles to a right onto Lake Warren Road at the sign for Lake Warren SP. Travel for 1.3 miles to the entrance to the park on the right.
GPS coordinates: N32 50.034 / W81 09.805
Maps: *DeLorme: South Carolina Atlas and Gazetteer* page 58, A2
About the campground: This peaceful, family-oriented park with picnic shelters and a community building is found along the banks of Lake George Warren. The serenity of the lake is astounding, and the park has provided a wonderful pier with a gazebo at the far end. There are two boat ramps and boat rentals are available, but the lake is limited to boats with a 10 horsepower motor or less. You can try your hand at fishing if you have a South Carolina state fishing license, but there's no swimming allowed. Take a stroll on one of two nature trails, or take advantage of the park's large open field where you could easily get a game of kickball together. The park has a wonderful program where you can borrow a Frisbee or a ball to toss around. As for the campground, it was designed for group camping, but if the campground is vacant, individuals are welcome as well. Reservations are required and must be made by contacting the park directly.

Barnwell Area

Campground	Total sites	Hookup sites	Max. RV length	Hookups	Toilets	Showers	Drinking water	Dump station	Recreation	Fee	Reservations
25 **Barnwell State Park**	26	25	38'	E, W, S*	F	Y	Y	Y	H, S, F, B*, V, P	$$	Y

* See campground entry for specific information

25 Barnwell State Park

Location: 223 State Park Rd., Blackville; about 6 miles north of Barnwell, and about 9 miles west of Denmark
Season: Year-round
Sites: 25; 1 group camping area is also available and can accommodate up to 50 people; cabin rentals are also available
Maximum length: 38 feet

Tulips take full bloom in the springtime.

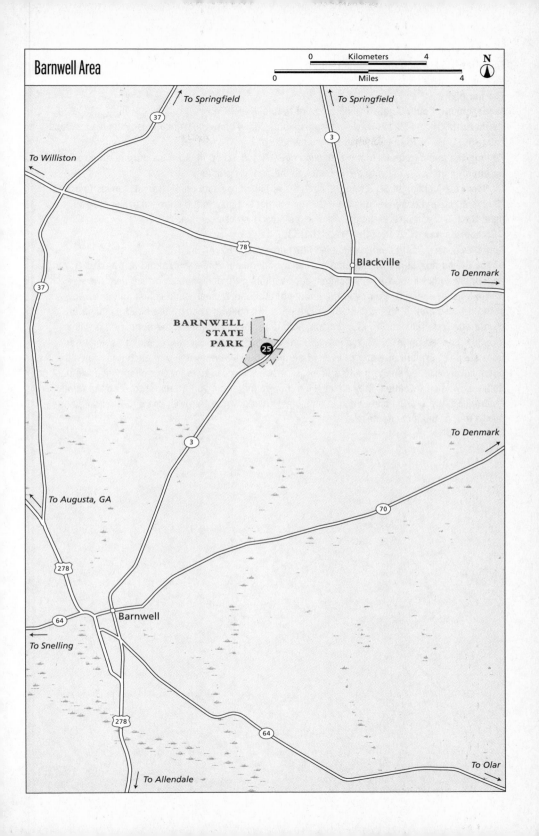

Barnwell Area

Kilometers
0   4
0   Miles   4

N

To Springfield
To Springfield

37

3

To Williston

78

Blackville

To Denmark

37

BARNWELL STATE PARK

25

To Denmark

3

To Augusta, GA

70

278

64

Barnwell

To Snelling

278

64

To Allendale

To Olar

Facilities: Flush toilets, hot showers, electric, water, fire rings, picnic tables, dump station, firewood for sale, pet friendly

Fee per night: $$

Management: South Carolina Department of Natural Resources

Contact: (803) 284-2212; www.southcarolinaparks.com/barnwell/camping.aspx; for reservations call (866) 345-7275 or visit www.reserveamerica.com

Finding the campground: From the junction of SC 3 and SC 70 in Barnwell, drive north on SC 3 for approximately 7.0 miles to the entrance to the park on your left.

From the junction of SC 3 and US 78 in Blackville, drive south on SC 3 for 1.7 miles to a stop sign. Turn left, and continue to follow SC 3 for another 0.9 mile to the entrance to the park on your right. Note: The entrance to the park sneaks up on you, so use caution.

GPS coordinates: N33 19.743 / W81 18.083

Maps: *DeLorme: South Carolina Atlas and Gazetteer* page 52, A4

About the campground: Sitting atop a small, wooded knoll, the campground at Barnwell State Park offers somewhat private campsites, each with its own picnic table and fire ring. There's also a large community fire ring in the middle of the loop. A small pond is just minutes away in the day-use area of this quaint, 307-acre park. Two spillways accent the pond as miniature man-made waterfalls easing your tension. A floating dock also adorns the pond, and a swim area just opened up in 2013. You can launch your own canoe or kayak, or rent a fishing boat from the park. Explore by water or by land on the 1.5-mile nature trail that circumnavigates the pond. Lovely wooded shelters with a fireplace inside allow you to enjoy this charming state park during any type of weather. They also have a playground and a volleyball net to keep the family entertained. If you appreciate historic buildings, head down to Barnwell or up to Blackville and take a tour of the local heritage.

Aiken Area

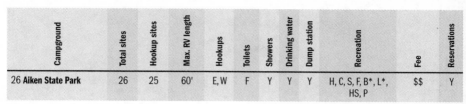

Campground	Total sites	Hookup sites	Max. RV length	Hookups	Toilets	Showers	Drinking water	Dump station	Recreation	Fee	Reservations
26 Aiken State Park	26	25	60'	E, W	F	Y	Y	Y	H, C, S, F, B*, L*, HS, P	$$	Y

* See campground entry for specific information

26 Aiken State Park

Location: 1145 State Park Rd., Windsor; about 12 miles east of Aiken, and about 35 miles west of Orangeburg

Season: Year-round

Sites: 25; 1 group camping area is also available, and can accommodate up to 30 people

Maximum Length: 60 feet; but there are a limited number of sites that can accommodate this size RV

Facilities: Flush toilets, hot showers, electric, water, fire rings, picnic tables, lantern holders, tent pads on some sites, dump station, firewood for sale, pet friendly

Fee per night: $$

Management: South Carolina Department of Natural Resources

Contact: (803) 649-2857; www.southcarolinaparks.com/aiken/camping.aspx; for reservations call (866) 345-7275 or visit www.reserveamerica.com

Finding the campground: From the junction of US 78 and SC 781 near Williston, drive northwest on US 78 for 5.3 miles to a right turn onto State Park Road (SR 53), at the sign for Aiken State Natural Area. Follow State Park Road for 5.0 miles to a left onto Old Tory Trail (SR 1669). Travel for less than 0.1 mile to the entrance to the park on your right.

From the junction of SC 4 and SC 302 near Aiken, drive south on State Park Road (SR 53, across from SC 302), for 2.0 miles to a right turn onto Old Tory Trail and follow the directions above.

GPS coordinates: N33 33.084 / W81 29.421

Maps: *DeLorme: South Carolina Atlas and Gazetteer* page 44, E2

About the campground: Acre upon acre of rolling horse pastures surround the Aiken area, and the South Fork of the Edisto River skirts across the northern portion of the park. A loop road leads you through this wooded wonderland and is long enough to cycle on. Almost every one of the twenty-five campsites sits along the perimeter of a flat longleaf pine forest, giving you a little more privacy than most other state parks in the Piedmont. Aiken State Park stays busy throughout the week, and for good reason. There are two lakes, two ponds, a canoe

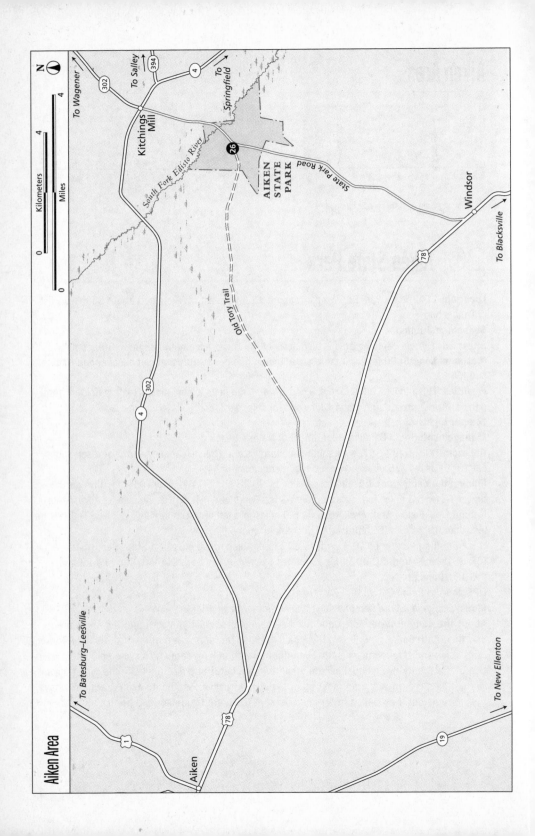

Aiken Area

Relax and enjoy the view at Aiken State Park.

launch, and hiking trails that traverse the entire 1,000-plus-acre park. They have canoe rentals, and even offer a shuttle service for paddlers, so you can feel free to explore the Edisto River at your leisure. A swim area is open seasonally, and horseshoe pits are also available. Whether you picnic by the pond, or visit one of the three artesian wells on the property, you're sure to enjoy your stay. For an evening outing, visit the Dupont Planetarium in downtown Aiken.

Aiken to North Augusta Area

	Campground	Total sites	Hookup sites	Max. RV length	Hookups	Toilets	Showers	Drinking water	Dump station	Recreation	Fee	Reservations
27	**Boyd Pond County Park**	**	0	n/a	n/a	F	N	Y*	N	H, M, F, B*, L, P, **	No Fee	Y
28	**Langley Pond County Park**	**	0	n/a	n/a	F	N	N	N	S, F, B, L, P	No Fee	Y

* See campground entry for specific information

27 Boyd Pond County Park

Location: 373 Boyd Pond Rd., Aiken; about 5 miles southwest of Aiken
Season: Year-round
Sites: Open area, no set designated sites
Maximum length: n/a
Facilities: Flush toilets, water fountain, pet friendly
Fee per night: No fee
Management: Aiken County Parks and Recreation Commission
Contact: (803) 642-0314; www.aikencountysc.gov/tourism/bpp.htm
Finding the campground: From the junction of SC 302 and SC 118 in Aiken, drive south on SC 302 for 6.2 miles to a right onto Boyd Pond Road at the sign for Boyd Pond Park and travel for 1.4 miles to the park on your right.

From the junction of SC 302 and US 278 in Hollow Creek, drive north on SC 302 for approximately 2.8 miles to a left onto Boyd Pond Road and travel for 1.4 miles to the park on your right.

This longhorn bull keeps onlookers at a distance

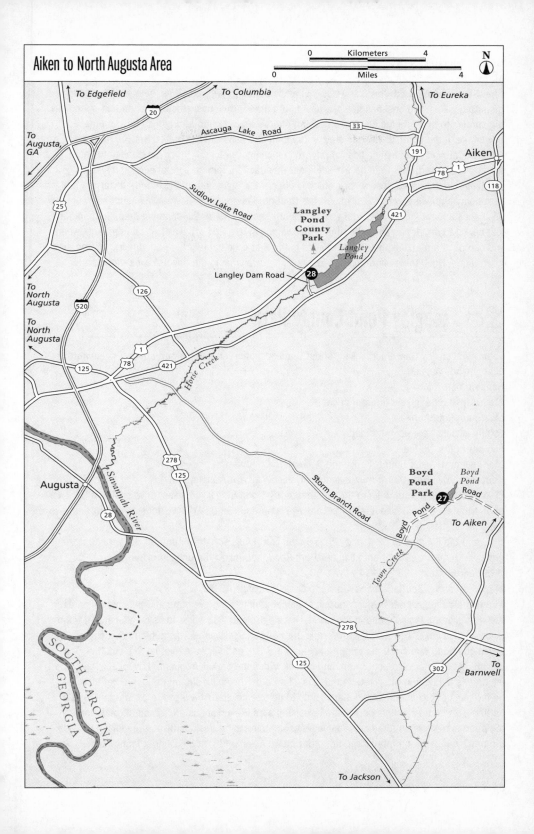

Aiken to North Augusta Area

Kilometers 0 — 4

Miles 0 — 4

N

To Edgefield

To Columbia

To Eureka

20

To Augusta, GA

Ascauga Lake Road

33

191

Aiken

78

1

25

Sudlow Lake Road

118

Langley Pond County Park

Langley Pond

421

Langley Dam Road

28

126

520

To North Augusta

Horse Creek

1

To North Augusta

78

421

125

278

125

Storm Branch Road

Boyd Pond Park

Boyd Pond Road

27

Augusta

Savannah River

Boyd Pond

To Aiken

28

Town Creek

SOUTH CAROLINA

GEORGIA

278

125

302

To Barnwell

To Jackson

GPS coordinates: N33 27.119 / W81 47.791
Maps: *DeLorme: South Carolina Atlas and Gazetteer* page 43, G8
About the campground: This Aiken County Park is brimming with activities. Trails for hiking and mountain biking, two baseball fields, a health and fitness trail, basketball hoop, and an open field big enough to fly a kite are just the beginning. There's a boat ramp and a dock for you to take full advantage of the pond, or you can stay on dry land and fish from the banks. But you must have a South Carolina state fishing license prior to launching your lure. If that's not enough to keep the family amused, they even have a small dirt racetrack for remote control cars, and star gazers delight in the park's observatory, which is open a few nights out of the month. If you're a real astronomy enthusiast, you can also visit the Dupont Planetarium in downtown Aiken. The park itself sees a lot of local traffic, and you can clearly see why. As for the camping area, the park has just begun to develop it, so at the time of this writing in late 2013, it was just an open area where you can pitch a tent. I expect this to change in the future, so contact the park directly for updated information. Flush toilets and drinking fountains are available in the day-use area of the park.

28 Langley Pond County Park

Location: Langley Dam Road, Aiken; about 5 miles southwest of Aiken and about 5 miles northeast of North Augusta
Season: Year-round
Sites: Open area, no set number of sites
Maximum length: n/a
Facilities: Flush toilets, pet friendly
Fee per night: No fee
Management: Aiken County Parks and Recreation Commission
Contact: (803) 642-0314; www.aikencountysc.gov/tourism/langley.htm
Finding the campground: From the junction of US 1 and SC 191 in Aiken, drive south on US 1 for approximately 2.9 miles to a left onto Langley Dam Road (SR 254). Travel for less than 0.1 mile to the park on the left.

From the junction of US 1 and US 278 near North Augusta, drive north on US 1 for approximately 3.3 miles to a right onto Langley Dam Road, and follow the directions above.
GPS coordinates: N33 31.434 / W81 50.810
Maps: *DeLorme: South Carolina Atlas and Gazetteer* page 43, F8
About the campground: This very populated local park has a playground and picnic pavilion near the shores of the largest pond in the world. That's right, with 285 acres to its credit, Langley Pond is just inches shy of being a lake, making it the world's largest pond. This petite park alongside the enormous pond offers you the opportunity to swim, fish, paddle, water-ski, Jet Ski, etc. There's a designated swim area, a boat ramp, and a dock. While the park is frequented by locals, the camping area is a little-known secret. Camping is allowed on the south side of the pond, but there are no fire rings or picnic tables and there's little to no tree cover. Just a place to pitch a tent, and a bathhouse with flush toilets only near the parking area. Reservations are required. Quite honestly, the pond is pleasing, but the camping leaves something to be desired. If you are looking for a day trip that's out of the ordinary, head up to downtown Aiken and visit the Dupont Plantarium.

Edgefield & J. Strom Thurmond Lake

Campground	Total sites	Hookup sites	Max. RV length	Hookups	Toilets	Showers	Drinking water	Dump station	Recreation	Fee	Reservations
29 Lick Fork Lake Campground	9	0	40'	N	V, F	Y	Y	Y	H, M, S*, F, B*, L* P	$	N
30 Modoc Campground	70	69	48'	E, W	F	Y	Y	Y	H*, M*, S, F, B, L, P	$$-$$$	Y
31 Hamilton Branch State Park	188	171	40'	E, W	F	Y	Y	Y	H, M, S, F, B, L, P	$$-$$$	Y

* See campground entry for specific information

29 Lick Fork Lake Campground

Location: About 10 miles southwest of Edgefield, and about 12 miles north of North Augusta
Season: May 1–November 15
Sites: 9
Maximum length: 40 feet
Facilities: Vault toilet, flush toilets in day-use area only, water spigots dispersed, fire rings, picnic tables, lantern holders, pet friendly
Fee per night: $
Management: Sumter National Forest–Long Cane District
Contact: (803) 637-5396; www.fs.usda.gov/recarea/scnfs/recreation/camping-cabins/recarea/?recid=47183&actid=29
Finding the campground: From I-20 near North Augusta, get off at exit 1 and drive north on SC 230 for 16.6 miles to a right onto Lick Fork Lake Road (SR 263) at the sign for Lick Fork Lake Recreation Area. Follow Lick Fork Lake Road for 1.9 miles to the entrance to the campground on the right.
     From the junction of SC 230 and SC 23 west of Edgefield, drive south on SC 230 for 0.3 mile to a left onto Lick Fork Lake Road (SR 263) and follow the directions above.
GPS coordinates: N33 43.897 / W82 02.175
Maps: *DeLorme: South Carolina Atlas and Gazetteer* page 42, B5
About the campground: Horses, cattle, and even goats fill the countryside as you travel through the Sumter National Forest on your way to Lick Fork Lake. The picnic area here is easily one of the nicest ones I've seen in the state. Stone walls create tiers of tables and grills overlooking the lush green grass in the swim area. While the day-use area and campground stay open through mid-November, the swim area closes October 1. The lake itself is brown in color but very inviting and can be enjoyed either by land or by water. A 2-mile hiking trail loops around the lake, or you can launch a canoe or kayak and explore it in its entirety. The Horn Creek Trail is also located within the recreation area and is open to hikers and mountain bikers. If you're an avid mountain biker, I recommend you head down the road a bit farther and explore the Forks Area Trail System, known

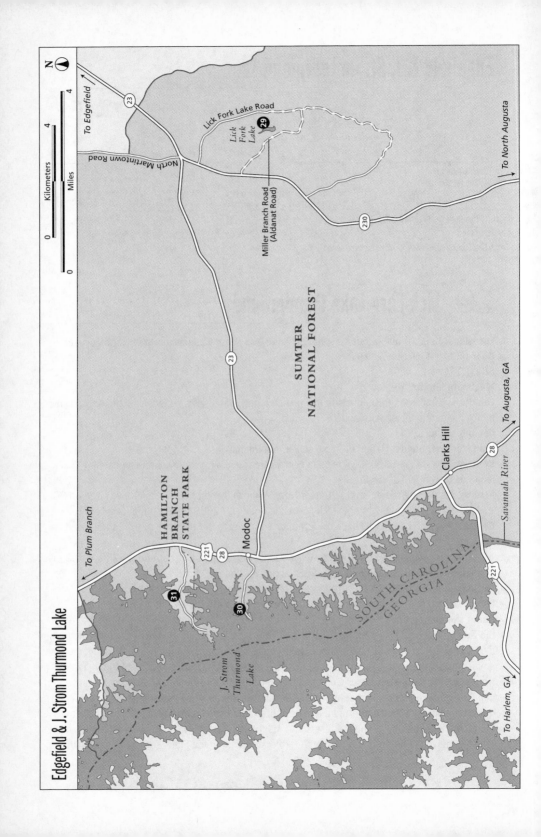

Edgefield & J. Strom Thurmond Lake

Mikey watches the geese swim by on Lick Fork Lake.

to the locals as FATS. As for the campground, it's wooded, offering campers privacy, but there are vault toilets and no showers. Most importantly, this area is subject to closure, so be sure to call ahead. If you are ready for a break from the forest, head over to the town of Edgefield. They have wonderful antique shops, historic pre-war homes, and the town is on the National Register of Historic Places.

30 Modoc Campground

Location: 296 Modoc Camp Rd., Modoc; about 15 miles south of McCormick, and about 15 miles north of Augusta, Georgia
Season: Mar 30–Sept 30
Sites: 7
Maximum length: 48 feet, but there are a limited number of sites that can accommodate this size RV
Facilities: Flush toilets, hot showers, electric, water, fire rings, charcoal grills, picnic tables, lantern holders, dump station, pet friendly
Fee per night: $$–$$$
Management: US Army Corps of Engineers
Contact: (864) 333-2272; www.sas.usace.army.mil/About/DivisionsandOffices/Operations Division/JStromThurmondDamandLake/PlanaVisit/Camping.aspx; for reservations, call (877) 444-6777 or visit www.recreation.gov

One of the Army Corps of Engineers' typical courtesy docks can be found at Modoc Campground

Finding the campground: From the junction of US 221 and SC 23 in Modoc, drive south on US 221 for 0.2 mile to a right onto Modoc Camp Road at the sign for Modoc Campground and travel for 0.5 mile to the campground.

From the junction of US 221 and SC 28 in Clarks Hill, drive north on US 221 for approximately 3.3 miles to a left onto Modoc Camp Road and follow the directions above.

GPS coordinates: N33 43.465 / W82 12.915

Maps: *DeLorme: South Carolina Atlas and Gazetteer* page 42, C3

About the campground: Four loops comprise this lakeside campground. Once again, the Army Corps of Engineers has outdone itself. With site after site along the shores of J. Strom Thurmond Lake, the location and view are astonishing. You can launch your boat on the property and cruise right up to the edge of your campsite for easier access to the lake. Along with the boat ramp is the typical courtesy dock seen in most all of the Army Corps campgrounds within the state. Swim, fish, boat, paddle, Jet Ski, water-ski. Whatever you fancy, the water awaits. Or, if you prefer to keep your feet dry, head down the road a bit and explore the Forks Area Trail System (FATS) on your mountain bike or on foot. With so much to do, and amazing scenery, Modoc lands itself on the Author's Favorites list.

31 Hamilton Branch State Park

Location: 111 Campground Rd., Plum Branch; about 12 miles south of McCormick and about 19 miles north of Augusta, Georgia
Season: Year-round
Sites: 171; 13 tent sites; 4 group camping areas are also available and can accommodate up to 100 people
Maximum length: 40 feet, but there are a limited number of sites that can accommodate this size RV
Facilities: Flush toilets, hot showers, electric, water, fire rings, picnic tables, dump station, pet friendly
Fee per night: $$–$$$
Management: South Carolina Department of Natural Resources
Contact: (864) 333-2223; www.southcarolinaparks.com/hamiltonbranch/camping.aspx; for reservations call (866) 345-7275 or visit www.reserveamerica.com

A perfect way to end the day.

Hamilton Branch offers stunning sunsets.

Finding the campground: From the junction of US 221 and SC 23 in Modoc, drive north on US 221 for 1.7 miles to the entrance to the park on your left.

From the junction of US 221 and US 378 in McCormick, drive south on US 221 for 12.3 miles to the entrance to the park on the right.

GPS coordinates: N33 45.254 / W82 12.202

Maps: *DeLorme: South Carolina Atlas and Gazetteer* page 42, B3

About the campground: Stars brightly shine overhead as you sit on the shores of J. Strom Thurmond Lake and gaze at the horizon. Campsite after glorious campsite rests upon the banks of this 71,000-acre lake, while the waves gently lap upon the land. Although it fills up on the weekends, the sites are very well spaced, so you don't notice the intrusion too much. Several loops make up the campground, and each loop sits on its own peninsula, jutting out into the water. With this in mind, remember that sound travels over water, so be sure to respect your neighbors, especially after the quiet hours of 10 p.m. Hiking and mountain biking can be enjoyed within the park along the Steven's Creek Bike Trail, or you can head out to the neighboring Sumter National Forest for many more miles of trails to explore. With spectacular sunrises and sunsets and waterfront camping, Hamilton Branch sits high up on the Author's Favorites list. The park has two boat ramps so you can easily access the lake. Swimming is permitted at your own risk, and you are allowed to fish provided you have a South Carolina state fishing license. Bring your binoculars along, because the area has some outstanding bird-watching opportunities, and if you're lucky, you may even spy an osprey or bald eagle soaring overhead.

McCormick & J. Strom Thurmond Lake

Campground	Total sites	Hookup sites	Max. RV length	Hookups	Toilets	Showers	Drinking water	Dump station	Recreation	Fee	Reservations
32 Hawe Creek Campground	34	34	45'	E, W	F	Y	Y	Y	S, F, B, L, P	$$$	Y
33 Baker Creek State Park	101	50	54'	E, W	F	Y	Y	Y	H, M, S, F, B, L, V, G*, P	$$-$$$	Y
34 Hickory Knob State Resort Park	44	44	80'	E, W	F	Y	Y	Y	H, M, S, F, B, L, A, BB, G, T, V, P, **	$$	Y
35 Morrow Bridge Seasonal Camp	31	0	40'	N	N	N	N	N	H, O	$	N
36 LeRoys Ferry Campground	10	0	None	N	V	N	Y*	N	F, B, L	$	N
37 Mt. Carmel Campground	44	39	40'	E, W	F	Y	Y	Y	S, F, B, L, P	$$-$$$	Y

* See campground entry for specific information

32 Hawe Creek Campground

Location: 1505 Chamberlains Ferry Rd., McCormick; about 7 miles southwest of McCormick
Season: Mar 30–Sept 30
Sites: 34
Maximum length: 45 feet
Facilities: Flush toilets, hot showers, electric, water, fire rings, picnic tables, lantern holders, dump station, pet friendly
Fee per night: $$$
Management: US Army Corps of Engineers
Contact: (864) 443-5441; www.sas.usace.army.mil/About/DivisionsandOffices/Operations Division/JStromThurmondDamandLake/PlanaVisit/Camping/CampingInformation.aspx; for reservations, call (877) 444-6777 or visit www.recreation.gov.
Finding the campground: From the junction of US 378 and US 221 in McCormick, drive west on US 378 for 2.7 miles to a left onto Chamberlains Ferry Road (SR 124) and travel for 3.5 miles to where the road ends at the entrance to the campground.
From the junction of US 378 and the South Carolina/Georgia state line, drive east on US 378 for 3.9 miles to a right onto Chamberlains Ferry Road (SR 124) and follow directions above.
GPS coordinates: N33 50.443 / W82 20.155
Maps: *DeLorme: South Carolina Atlas and Gazetteer* page 42, A2 & 33, H7
About the campground: Talk about privacy! The Army Corps of Engineers really outdid themselves here, easily landing Hawe Creek among the Author's Favorites. The sites are so well spaced out, I'm taken aback in the best of ways. Most of the campsites sit upon little ledges overlooking the

McCormick & J. Strom Thurmond Lake

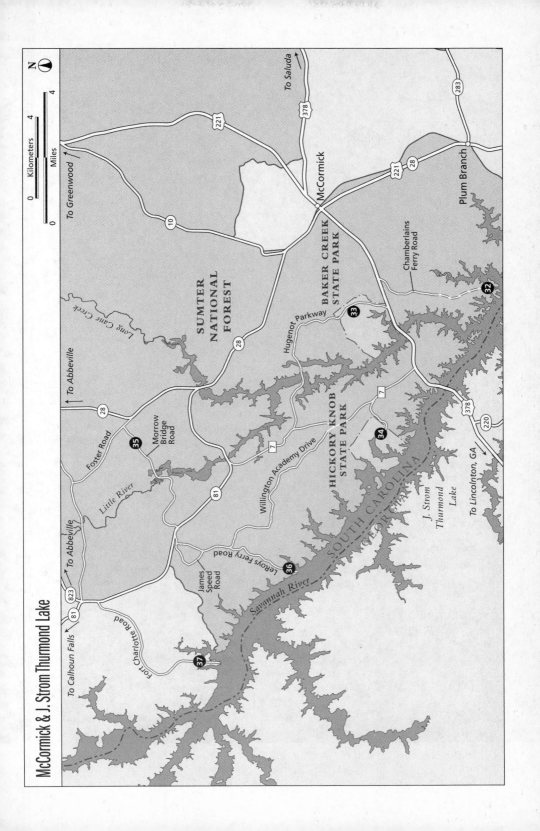

A giant root burl takes up half of this tree trunk.

water's edge with amazing sunset views at the ready. Boaters and land lovers alike are sure to enjoy this one. There's a narrow boat ramp, a courtesy dock, and you can cruise your craft right up to the shore alongside some of the sites. As if that's not enough, the Dorn Boating and Sportfishing Facility is just a mile up the road.

33 Baker Creek State Park

Location: 863 Baker Creek Rd., McCormick; about 3 miles southwest of McCormick and 2 miles northeast of the South Carolina/Georgia state line
Season: Mar 1–Sept 30
Sites: 100; 1 group camp area is also available and can accommodate up to 100 people
Maximum length: 54 feet
Facilities: Flush toilets, hot showers, electric, water, some sites have fire rings, charcoal grills, picnic tables, dump station, pet friendly
Fee per night: $$–$$$
Management: South Carolina Department of Natural Resources
Contact: (864) 443-2457; www.southcarolinaparks.com/bakercreek/camping.aspx; for reservations call (866) 345-7275, visit www.reserveamerica.com, or call Baker Creek's sister park Hickory Knob State Resort Park at (864) 391-2450
Finding the campground: From the junction of US 378 and US 221 in McCormick, drive west on US 378 for 3.7 miles to a right onto Hugenot Parkway (SR 467) at the sign for Baker Creek State Park. Travel for 1.1 miles to a left onto Baker Creek Road at the entrance to the park.
    From the South Carolina/Georgia state line and US 378, drive east on US 378 for 2.9 miles to a left onto Hugenot Parkway and follow the directions above.
GPS coordinates: N33 53.865 / W82 20.924
Maps: *DeLorme: South Carolina Atlas and Gazetteer* page 33, H7
About the campground: Resting near the mouth of Baker Creek as it widens up into the Little River lies Baker Creek State Park. The park has two distinct campgrounds, and a group camping area as well. Campground #1 is dedicated to tent campers, and the sites in this loop have dispersed water spigots but no electric hookups. Site after site sits upon the water's edge, but they are a bit close together. Luckily, this area is less populated, so these tight quarters seem a little less obvious. Campground #2 is open to all campers, but has even less privacy than the first. Even the nicest waterfront campsite in this loop is close to your neighbors. These sites have charcoal grills, but only a few have the traditional fire ring. I will say that whatever these campgrounds lack in privacy, the park makes up for with its pristine location and a slew of on-site activities. There are two boat ramps, one by the campground and the other at a remote location near the park. Launch your boat and explore the far reaches of the Little River Blueway, or cruise your boat right up to your campsite. Fish from the banks or the boat, provided you have a South Carolina state fishing license, or take a quick dip to cool down after a day on the trail. That's right, Baker's Creek State Park isn't just for boaters. Land lovers can enjoy miles of hiking and mountain bike trails all contained within the park. Sit and relax on the lovely deck overlooking the river, or head up the road to her sister park Hickory Knob, and hit the links on their 18-hole championship golf course.

34 Hickory Knob State Resort Park

Location: 1591 Resort Dr., McCormick; about 8 miles west of McCormick
Season: Year-round
Sites: 44; cabin rentals and lodge rooms are also available
Maximum Length: 80 feet
Facilities: Flush toilets, hot showers, electric, water, fire rings, picnic tables, dump station, pet friendly
Fee per night: $$
Management: South Carolina Department of Natural Resources
Contact: (864) 391-2450; www.southcarolinaparks.com/hickoryknob/camping.aspx; for reservations call (866) 345-7275 or visit www.reserveamerica.com
Finding the campground: From the junction of US 378 and US 221 in McCormick, drive west on US 378 for 5.8 miles to a right turn onto Highway 7 at the sign for Hickory Knob State Park. Follow Highway 7 for 1.6 miles to a left onto Resort Drive (SR 421) at the entrance to the park. Drive 1.3 miles to the campground on the left.

From the junction of US 378 and the South Carolina/Georgia state line, drive east on US 378 for 0.8 mile to a left turn onto Highway 7 and follow the directions above.

From the junction of SC 81 and SC 28 near McCormick, drive north on SC 81 for 1.7 miles to a left onto Highway 7 and travel for 5.2 miles to the entrance to the park on the right.
GPS coordinates: N33 53.008 / W82 24.893
Maps: *DeLorme: South Carolina Atlas and Gazetteer* page 33, H6
About the campground: Holy cow, this place has it all! Hickory Knob is touted as South Carolina's only State Resort Park, and you can clearly see why. You would think that its ideal location along the shores of J. Strom Thurmond Lake would be the biggest perk of the park, but that's just the beginning. Yes, they have a perfect waterfront locale, where you can swim, fish (South Carolina state fishing license required), use the boat ramp or dock, rent a canoe or kayak, or simply enjoy the fabulous views. But again, that's just a small taste. The park has nearly 12 miles of trails that you can either hike or mountain bike on, and a swimming pool to take a dip in after a long day on the trail. The gorgeous 18-hole championship golf course is definitely a highlight, with a driving range, practice greens, and a pro shop to accompany it. They have the customary sports of basketball, volleyball, and tennis, but much to my amazement, they also have an archery and skeet shooting range as well. There's a convention center, restaurant, gift shop, and lodge, but personally, I prefer the comfort of my tent over a lodge room. The campground is separated from the day-use area and sits across a small cove in the lake from the main body of the park. Campsites rest just above the shoreline, and surprisingly, for such a large park, the campground is small, wooded, and intimate. The sites are well-spaced but narrow, and although the area is wooded, it's not necessarily shady. All of the park's amenities are within easy reach, yet you still have that authentic camping feel. If for some reason you need more to do, take a jaunt over to the town of McCormick and visit the historic Dorn Mill & Gin, or take a tour of the Heritage Gold Mine Park.

A white heron treads softly as he patiently waits for his prey.

35 Morrow Bridge Seasonal Camp

Location: About 15 miles south of Abbeville, and about 10 miles northwest of McCormick
Season: Sept 14–Jan 4
Sites: 31
Maximum length: 40 feet
Facilities: No toilets, no water, a few primitive fire rings, pet friendly
Fee per night: $
Management: Sumter National Forest–Long Cane District
Contact: (803) 637-5396; www.fs.usda.gov/recarea/scnfs/recreation/camping-cabins/recarea/?recid=47185&actid=29
Finding the campground: From the junction of SC 28 and SC 81 near McCormick, drive north on SC 28 for 1.7 miles to a left onto Foster Road (SR 37). Follow Foster Road for 0.4 mile to a left onto Morrow Bridge Road (SR 39) and travel for 0.5 mile to the campground on the left.

From the junction of SC 28 and SC 81 near McCormick, drive north on SC 81 for 1.7 miles to a right onto Forest Road 3015 (FR 3015, just across from Highway 7). Follow FR 3015 for 2.6 miles to where it ends. Turn right, and travel for 1.7 miles to the campground on the right.

From the junction of SC 28 and SC 72 near Abbeville, drive south on SC 28 for approximately 12.0 miles to a right onto Foster Road (SR 37) and follow the directions above.
GPS coordinates: N33 59.417 / W82 25.238
Maps: *DeLorme: South Carolina Atlas and Gazetteer* page 33, F8
About the campground: A single small loop makes up this seasonal hunt camp. The sites rest amid the longleaf pines and are flat and fairly close together. Except for the occasional primitive fire ring here and there, there are no other amenities on the campsites. Designed primarily for hunters, this camp is only open a few months out of the year, so keep this in mind when you plan to camp here. Also, be sure to come prepared, as there is no water supply and no bathroom facilities anywhere on the property. The surrounding forest is abundant with wildlife and has miles of hiking and off-road vehicle trails. Maps are available at the Long Cane Ranger Station in Edgefield.

36 LeRoys Ferry Campground

Location: On the eastern bank of J. Strom Thurmond Lake, about 15 miles west of McCormick and about 5 miles south of Willington
Season: Year-round
Sites: 10
Maximum length: None
Facilities: Vault toilets, water (near the park entrance), fire rings, charcoal grills, picnic tables, lantern holders, trash cans, pet friendly
Fee per night: $
Management: US Army Corps of Engineers
Contact: (800) 533-3478; www.sas.usace.army.mil/About/DivisionsandOffices/Operations Division/JStromThurmondDamandLake/PlanaVisit/Camping.aspx; for reservations, call (877) 444-6777 or visit www.recreation.gov.

Man and nature unite alongside a country road.

Finding the campground: From the junction of SC 81 and SC 28 near McCormick, drive north on SC 81 for 4.4 miles to a left onto James Speed Road (SR 60) at the sign for LeRoys Ferry Campground. Travel for 50 feet and turn right, continuing to follow James Speed Road for another 0.5 mile to a left onto Willington Academy Drive (SR 135) at the sign for LeRoys Ferry Campground. Travel for 1.6 miles and veer right onto Leroys Ferry Road (SR 366). Follow Leroys Ferry Road for approximately 2.0 miles to the campground.

GPS coordinates: N33 55.372 / W82 29.312

Maps: *DeLorme: South Carolina Atlas and Gazetteer* page 32, G5

About the campground: Well off the beaten path, LeRoys Ferry is unlike any other Army Corps of Engineers campground in the state. The unmanned entrance has a self-pay station, which is based on the honor system, so be sure to bring exact change. The sites are large, comparatively far apart, and right on the water's edge. With a steep and deep boat launch on the property, you can bring your boat along and cruise it right up to your campsite. The camping is fairly primitive, with a vault toilet, and no water or electric hookups. There is, however, a single hand water pump that sits behind the self-pay station near the entrance to the campground. This is a good distance away from the campsites, so you may want to bring plenty of drinking water along. If you're not in need of creature comforts, this is a great place to get away from it all, especially if you're a boat owner. With a 1,200-mile shoreline, J. Strom Thurmond Lake is one of the largest public recreation lakes in the southeast, and it's just waiting for you to explore.

37 Mt. Carmel Campground

Location: 2926 Fort Charlotte Rd., Mt. Carmel; about 20 miles southwest of Abbeville, and about 22 miles northwest of McCormick

Season: Mar 30–Sept 2

Sites: 44

Maximum length: 40 feet, but there are a limited number of sites that can accommodate this size RV

Facilities: Flush toilets, hot showers, electric, water, fire rings, picnic tables, fish cleaning tables, lantern holders, dump station, pet friendly

Fee per night: $$–$$$

Management: US Army Corps of Engineers

Contact: (864) 391-2711; www.sas.usace.army.mil/About/DivisionsandOffices/Operations Division/JStromThurmondDamandLake/PlanaVisit/Camping.aspx www.sas.usace.army.mil/lakes/thurmond/camping.html; for reservations, call (877) 444-6777 or visit www.recreation.gov

Finding the campground: From the junction of SC 81 and SC 823 in Mt. Carmel, drive south on SC 81 for 0.4 mile to a right onto Fort Charlotte Road (SR 91) and travel for 4.5 miles to the entrance to the campground at the end of the road.

From the junction of SC 81 and SC 28 near McCormick, drive north on SC 81 for 8.1 miles to a hard left onto Fort Charlotte Road (SR 91) at the sign for Mt. Carmel Campground and follow the directions above.

GPS coordinates: N33 57.679 / W82 32.334

Maps: *DeLorme: South Carolina Atlas and Gazetteer* page 32, G4

Mt. Carmel offers pristine waterfront camping.

About the campground: Trees and distance separate campers as they enjoy lakeside camping at its best. This wonderful, well-marked facility has easily made its way onto the Author's Favorites list. The campsites are very well spaced, offering lots of privacy to RV and tent campers alike. One of the two boat ramps is dedicated to campers only, and there's a silver courtesy dock, as is typical of the Army Corps of Engineers campgrounds. You can anchor your boat right alongside your campsite, and enjoy fishing, swimming, and boating as you explore the far northern reaches of J. Strom Thurmond Lake. Each campsite has a fish cleaning table, so you can catch, clean, and cook your dinner without ever leaving your home away from home. Note, you must have a South Carolina state fishing license prior to breaking out the rod and reel. If you plan to frequent the area, there's an RV/camper storage facility just up the road. Known locally as Hesters Bottom, Mt. Carmel holds historical significance from the American Revolution. Within the park you will notice interpretive placards educating visitors on the history of the area.

Calhoun Falls

Campground	Total sites	Hookup sites	Max. RV length	Hookups	Toilets	Showers	Drinking water	Dump station	Recreation	Fee	Reservations
38 **Calhoun Falls State Park**	100	86	60'	E, W	F	Y	Y	Y	H, S, F, B, L, T, BB, P	$$–$$$	Y

38 Calhoun Falls State Park

Location: 46 Maintenance Shop Rd., Calhoun Falls; about 16 miles east of Elberton, and about 15 miles west of Abbeville
Season: Year-round
Sites: 86; 14 rustic tent sites are also available
Maximum length: 40 feet
Facilities: Flush toilets, hot showers, electric, water, fire rings, picnic tables, lantern holders, dump station, ice and firewood for sale, laundry facility, pet friendly
Fee per night: $$–$$$
Management: South Carolina Department of Natural Resources
Contact: (864) 447-8267; www.southcarolinaparks.com/calhounfalls/camping.aspx; for reservations call (866) 345-7275 or visit www.reserveamerica.com
Finding the campground: From the junction of SC 81 and SC 72 in Calhoun Falls, drive north on SC 81 for 1.0 mile to a left onto CF State Park Road. Travel for 0.9 mile to the entrance to the park at the end of the road.

From the junction of SC 81 and SC 71 near Lowndesville, drive south on SC 81 for approximately 7.9 miles to a right onto Calhoun Falls State Park Road and follow the directions above.
GPS coordinates: N34 06.417 / W82 36.733
Maps: *DeLorme: South Carolina Atlas and Gazetteer* page 32, D4
About the campground: Wow! This facility is dressed to impress. Anglers flock to Calhoun Falls State Park, and it's easy to see why. Sitting at the southern reaches of Richard B. Russell Lake, the park has a prime location and has certainly made the most of it. As with most waterfront parks in the state, Calhoun Falls has a boat ramp, a seasonal swim beach, and two fishing piers. But this park also has a full-service marina, with an in-water fueling station, a tackle shop, fish cleaning station, and boat slips for long-term lease that include electric and water. As if this wasn't impressive enough, you can also rent a boat slip nightly, for the price of a campsite. As you enjoy the flawless waters of Lake Russell from your campsite, you have the added convenience of a slip to house your boat overnight. The park has two traditional campgrounds open to RVs and tents, and a third camping area dedicated for primitive tent campers only. The RV sites are wooded and spaced well apart from one another, giving everyone enough privacy, even on busy weekends. Although the lake is within view from most of the sites, trees and elevation form a natural barrier, keeping you from actually camping on the shoreline. All but one of the primitive tent sites is

Calhoun Falls

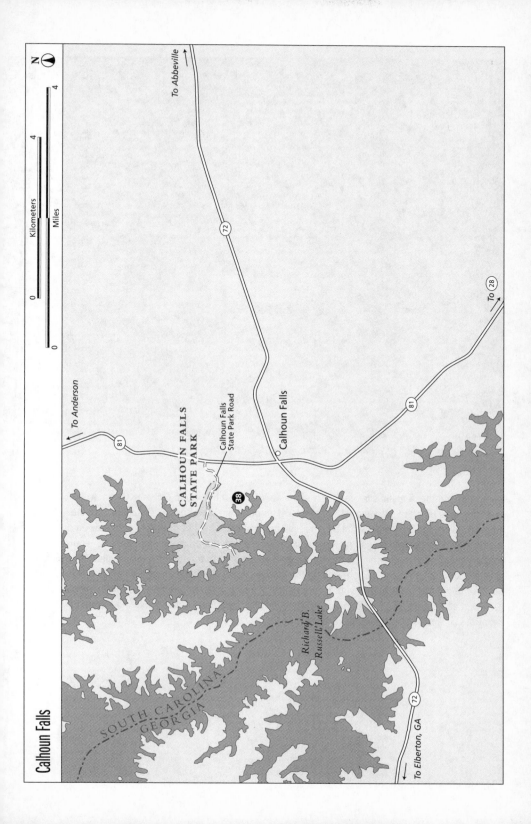

N

Kilometers
0   4

Miles
0   4

To Abbeville

72

To 28

To Anderson

81

CALHOUN FALLS STATE PARK

Calhoun Falls State Park Road

38

Calhoun Falls

81

Richard B. Russell Lake

SOUTH CAROLINA
GEORGIA

72

To Elberton, GA

Enjoy your own piece of paradise at Calhoun Falls State Park.

waterfront, but these rustic sites require a short walk from 30 feet up to 0.5 mile to reach. The tent sites sit a bit close to one another, and have an outdoor shower and flush toilets near the entrance to the loop. Clearly the lake is the high point of the park, but if you prefer to stay on dry land, the park has plenty for you as well. Hiking trails traverse the property, and there are tennis courts, a basketball net, picnic shelters, and playgrounds. And to top it all off, just across the lake near the town of Lowndesville, you will find the McCalla State Natural Area. McCalla has 10 miles worth of bridle trails that are open to hikers as well. A trail permit is required for those on horseback and can be obtained at the office in Calhoun Falls State Park. Riders must show proof of a negative Coggins test for their trusty steed.

Abbeville

Campground	Total sites	Hookup sites	Max. RV length	Hookups	Toilets	Showers	Drinking water	Dump station	Recreation	Fee	Reservations
39 **Parson's Mountain Campground**	23	0	40'	N	F	Y	Y	N	H, S*, F, B*, L*, O, P	$	N
40 **Fell Hunt and Horse Camp**	50	0	40'	N	V, F*	N	Y	N	H, M, R, O, P	$	N
41 **Midway Seasonal Camp**	**	0	None	N	V	N	N*	N	H, M, R, O, P	$	N

* See campground entry for specific information

39 Parson's Mountain Campground

Location: About 5 miles south of Abbeville, and about 15 miles north of McCormick
Season: May 1–Nov 15
Sites: 23
Maximum length: 40 feet
Facilities: Flush toilets, hot showers, water spigots dispersed, fire rings, picnic tables, lantern holders, pet friendly
Fee per night: $
Management: Sumter National Forest–Long Cane District
Contact: (803) 637-5396; www.fs.usda.gov/recarea/scnfs/recreation/camping-cabins/recarea/?recid=47187&actid=29
Finding the campground: From the junction of SC 28 and SC 81 near McCormick, drive north on SC 28 for approximately 11.6 miles to a right onto Parsons Mountain Road (SR 251) at the sign for Parson's Mountain and travel for 1.4 miles to the entrance to the campground on the right.

From the junction of SC 28 and SC 72 in Abbeville, drive south on SC 28 for 2.1 miles to a left onto Parsons Mountain Road (SR 251) at the sign for Parson's Mountain and follow the directions above.
GPS coordinates: N34 06.404 / W82 21.706
Maps: *DeLorme: South Carolina Atlas and Gazetteer* page 33, D7
About the campground: The name may be a bit deceiving, but Parson's Mountain is still the nicest national forest campground in the district. The mountain itself is actually an 800-foot peak that subtly stands out amid the recreation area. Two lovely picnic areas rest alongside a small, brown mountain lake. One is open to the public, while the other is dedicated for campers only. Several hiking trails traverse the area, and one even leads to the summit of Parson's Mountain itself. You can fish from the banks, or use the boat ramp to head out on the 28-acre lake. The launch and lake are open to nonmotorized boats only, and you must carry a South Carolina state fishing license if you plan on casting a line. There's a swim "beach" that closes on Oct 1, and the entire area is nicely wooded. If you prefer a bit faster pace than the peaceful setting of the picnic area, you can explore the expanse of the forest via the Parson's Mountain off-highway vehicle

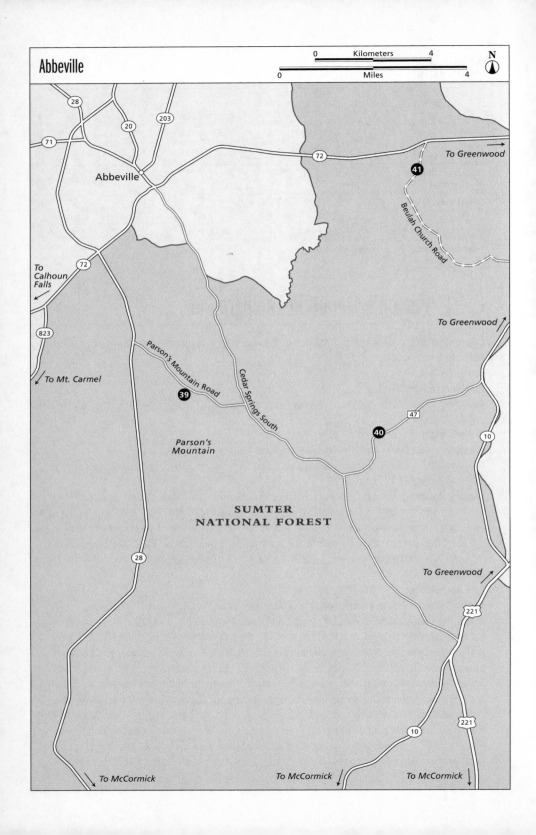

(OHV) trail. A nominal fee ($) and a permit are required to use the OHV trail. For a bit of culture, head up to Abbeville and see a play at the historic Abbeville Opera House.

40 Fell Hunt and Horse Camp

Location: About 7 miles southeast of Abbeville, and about 15 miles north of McCormick
Season: Year-round
Sites: 50
Maximum length: 40 feet
Facilities: Vault toilets, water spigots dispersed, primitive rock fire rings, pet friendly
Fee per night: $
Management: Sumter National Forest–Long Cane District
Contact: (803) 637-5396; www.fs.usda.gov/recarea/scnfs/recreation/camping-cabins/recarea/?recid=47181&actid=29
Finding the campground: From the junction of US 221 and SC 10 North in Bradley, drive south on US 221 for 2.0 miles to a right onto Cedar Springs South (SR 112) and travel for 4.6 miles to a right onto SR 47. Follow SR 47 for 1.5 miles to the entrance to the campground on the left.

From the junction of US 221 and SC 10 South near Bradley, drive north on US 221 for approximately 0.25 mile to a left onto Cedar Springs South (SR 112) and follow the directions above.

From the junction of SC 72 and SC 28 in Abbeville, drive east on SC 72 for approximately 2.0 miles to a right onto Main Street. After passing through town, Main Street becomes Cedar Springs South (SR 33). Follow this for approximately 8.3 miles (from SC 72) to a left onto SR 47. Follow SR 47 for 1.5 miles to the entrance to the campground on the left.
GPS coordinates: N34 05.675 / W82 17.239
Maps: *DeLorme: South Carolina Atlas and Gazetteer* page 33, E7
About the campground: The campsites at this 15-acre hunt and horse camp have the bare minimum on them, and with the old Cedar Springs Church and graveyard up the road, this area has an eerie feel about it. Stone fire rings are all that adorns the first thirty-four campsites. But at least these sites sit in a wooded area, and therefore provide plenty of shade. An open field makes up the remaining sixteen sites that comprise the horse camp portion of this primitive campground. These sites sit right next to one another and are lacking the simple stone fire rings that the hunt camp has. They do, however, have horse tie offs, and plenty of room for you to park your horse trailer. The Long Cane Horse Trailhead is on the property, so the benefit of this location is that it literally offers ride-in/ride-out camping. The diverse terrain

A bright red cardinal keeps a keen eye out.

of this 24-mile trail offers visitors a unique way to explore the forest. If hunting or horseback riding is not your thing, don't despair. The bridle trails are open to hikers as well. And the Parson's Mountain and Cedar Springs off-highway vehicle (OHV) trail systems are also within easy reach. As for mountain biking, the Forks Area Trail System, better known as FATS, sits at the far southern end of the Long Cane ranger district. This world-class trail system offers riders nearly 25 miles of epic adventure and is a must-do for mountain bikers of all skill levels. Although the campground doesn't have much to offer, the forest around it does. No matter which saddle you prefer, hop on and head out.

41 Midway Seasonal Camp

Location: About 7 miles east of Abbeville, and about 7 miles west of Greenwood
Season: Sept 14–Jan 4
Sites: 28
Maximum length: None
Facilities: Vault toilets, no water, pet friendly
Fee per night: $
Management: Sumter National Forest–Long Cane District
Contact: (803) 637-5396; www.fs.usda.gov/recarea/scnfs/recreation/camping-cabins/recarea/?recid=47185&actid=29
Finding the campground: From the junction of SC 72 and SC 28 in Abbeville, drive east on SC 72 for approximately 8.2 miles to a right onto Beulah Church Road and travel for 0.6 mile to the campground on the left.

From the junction of SC 72 and US 25 in Greenwood, drive west on SC 72 for approximately 5.8 miles to a left onto Beulah Church Road and travel for 0.6 mile to the campground on the left.

From the junction of SC 10 and US 221 in Bradley, drive north on SC 10 for 7.1 miles to a left onto Lorenzo Road. Follow Lorenzo Road, and after about 1.5 miles Lorenzo Road becomes Beulah Church Road. Continue on Beulah Church Road until you've gone 5.1 miles (from SC 10) to the campground on your right.
GPS coordinates: N34 10.754 / W82 16.531
Maps: *DeLorme: South Carolina Atlas and Gazetteer* page 33, C8
About the campground: Unless you're a die-hard hunter, skip this one. The campground at Midway is an open field, with posts marking your site, and that's about it. The sites are barely discernible from one another, and there's not a single amenity on them. No picnic tables, no lantern holders, and barely a primitive rock fire ring on the whole premises. A "sweet-smelling" vault toilet is all that Midway Camp has to offer. The water pump was broken at the time of this writing, and it's uncertain when, or if, they will repair it. So be sure to bring plenty of water along with the rest of your gear. The forest surrounding this seasonal camp is abundant with wildlife, and therefore this is primarily designed as a base camp for hunters. The upside for those of us that are not hunters is that there are trails nearby for just about every form of travel. Whether you hike, mountain bike, ride upon horseback, or prefer off-highway vehicle (OHV), you can find a trail to suit your needs within easy reach. Or, if you're looking for some civilization, head over to the town of Greenwood and visit the "Emerald Triangle." The area has something for you by day or by night. You can spend the day exploring the Museum and Railroad Historic Center and then enjoy a play at the Greenwood Community Theater by night.

Greenwood Area

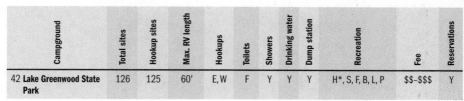

Campground	Total sites	Hookup sites	Max. RV length	Hookups	Toilets	Showers	Drinking water	Dump station	Recreation	Fee	Reservations
42 **Lake Greenwood State Park**	126	125	60'	E, W	F	Y	Y	Y	H*, S, F, B, L, P	$$-$$$	Y

* See campground entry for specific information

42 Lake Greenwood State Park

Location: 302 State Park Rd., Ninety Six; about 10 miles east of Greenwood, and about 25 miles southwest of Newberry

Season: Year-round

Sites: 125; 1 group camp area is also available and can accommodate up to 50 people

Maximum Length: 60 feet, but there are a limited number of sites that can accommodate this size RV

Facilities: Flush toilets, hot showers, electric, water, fire rings, picnic tables, dump station, firewood for sale, pet friendly

Fee per night: $$-$$$

Management: South Carolina Department of Natural Resources

Contact: (864) 543-3535; www.southcarolinaparks.com/lakegreenwood/camping.aspx; for reservations call (866) 345-7275 or visit www.reserveamerica.com

Finding the campground: From the junction of SC 702 and SC 246 near Ninety Six, drive east on SC 702 for approximately 5.3 miles to the entrance to the park on the left.

From the junction of SC 702 and SC 34 near Ninety Six, drive west on SC 702 for approximately 1.9 miles to the entrance to the park on the right.

GPS coordinates: N34 11.690 / W81 57.000

Maps: *DeLorme: South Carolina Atlas and Gazetteer* page 34, C1

About the campground: Wildflowers bloom during springtime, as wisteria and allamanda grow hand in hand, and sprays of daffodils pop up here and there. The contrast of colors is extraordinary! A dash of yellow mixed in with brilliant purple as the blossoms dangle down and line the trees throughout the park. It's no wonder that the aptly named Festival of Flowers Triathlon is held here every autumn. Originally developed by the Civilian Conservation Corps (CCC) back in the 1930s, the park now has an on-site "museum" full of historic CCC exhibits. The campground rests along the shores of Lake Greenwood and stays busy throughout the year. While the campsites seem a bit crowded, the park location and amenities help overcome the crowding. Two boat ramps allow you to access the lake, and you can cruise your craft right up to many of the campsites. You can fish from the park's pier or from the banks of the lake, as long as you have a South Carolina state fishing license. Also, this is one of the many state parks that participates in a tackle loaner program, meaning you can borrow a rod, reel, and tackle box if you don't have your own. Although there's no designated swim

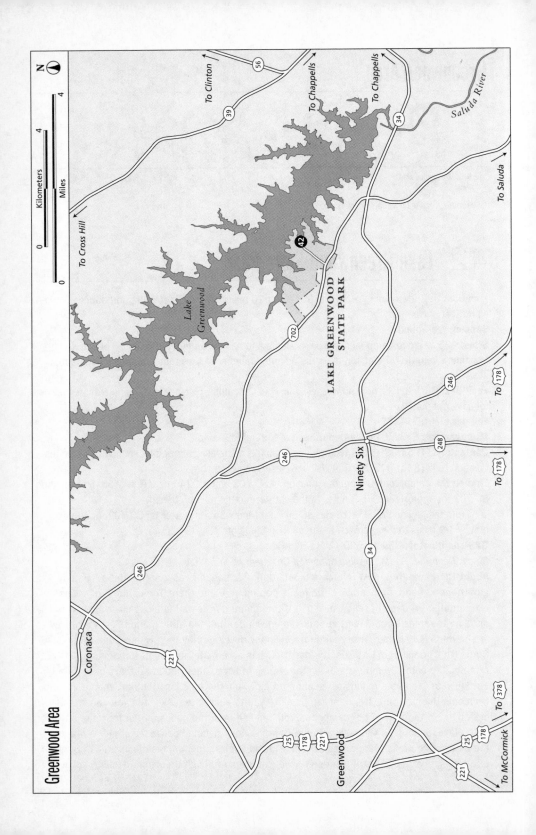

Greenwood Area

Wisteria flowers flourish in the springtime.

area, you can take a dip in the pristine waters of Lake Greenwood at your own risk. A 0.8-mile nature trail loops out and back, and gives you the opportunity for a quick hike. If you're a history buff, you may want to visit the National Historic Site in Ninety Six, or head over to Greenwood to take in a play at the community theater or check out the Museum and Railroad Historic Center.

Newberry Area

Campground	Total sites	Hookup sites	Max. RV length	Hookups	Toilets	Showers	Drinking water	Dump station	Recreation	Fee	Reservations
43 **Lynch's Woods County Park**	1	0	n/a	N	V*	N	N	N	H, M, R, P	No Fee	Y*
44 **Dreher Island State Park**	117	112	65'	E, W	F	Y	Y	Y	H, S, F, B, L, P	$$–$$$	Y

* See campground entry for specific information

43 Lynch's Woods County Park

Location: In the town of Newberry
Season: Year-round
Sites: 1 site can hold 3–4 tents
Maximum length: n/a
Facilities: Vault toilet (near park entrance), primitive fire rings, charcoal grill, picnic tables, pet friendly
Fee per night: None
Management: Newberry County Parks and Recreation
Contact: (803) 924-8328; www.newberry-college.net/chorn/Lynch's/Index.htm
Finding the campground: From the junction of US 76 and SC 391 in Prosperity, drive north on US 76 for 4.9 miles to a right onto Walter Cousins Road at the entrance to the park. Follow the one-way road through Lynch's Woods for approximately 1.0 mile to the campground on your left.

From I-26 near Newberry, get off at exit 76 and drive west on SC 219 for approximately 3.2 miles to a left onto US 76. Travel for 0.7 mile to a left onto Walter Cousins Road at the entrance to the park and follow the directions above.
GPS coordinates: N34 16.656 / W81 34.376
Maps: *DeLorme: South Carolina Atlas and Gazetteer* page 35, A6
About the campground: The 4-mile loop road rises and falls as it surrounds the lush green forest known as Lynch's Woods. A small muddy creek and some wet-weather tributaries snake their way through this perfect patch of paradise that sits tucked away in the sprawling town of Newberry. The campground has the bare minimum, simply a few flat spots to pitch a tent, and a special permit is required to light a campfire. Locals frequent Lynch's Woods on a regular basis, as it has several miles of well-groomed hiking and mountain bike trails. Horseback riding is also allowed on the main park road and on designated trails. A single vault toilet greets you near the park entrance, but this is a mile from the campground. Also, be advised that there is no potable water available, so be sure to come prepared and bring plenty of water with you. Although there is no fee, reservations are required, and a camping permit number can be obtained over the phone. Camping is limited to a 2-night maximum stay.

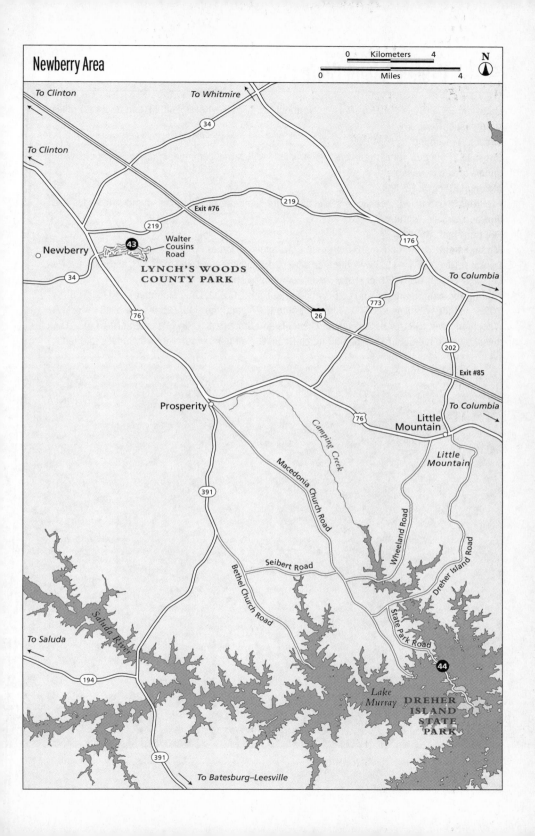

44 Dreher Island State Park

Location: 3677 State Park Rd., Prosperity; about 30 miles west of Columbia, and about 20 miles southeast of Newberry
Season: Year-round
Sites: 112; 5 group camp areas are also available and can accommodate up to 30 people; cabin rentals are also available
Maximum length: 65 feet
Facilities: Flush toilets, hot showers, electric, water, fire rings, picnic tables, dump station, ice and firewood for sale, pet friendly
Fee per night: $$-$$$
Management: South Carolina Department of Natural Resources
Contact: (803) 364-4152; www.southcarolinaparks.com/dreherisland/camping.aspx; for reservations call (866) 345-7275 or visit www.reserveamerica.com
Finding the campground: From I-26, get off at exit 85 (SC 202, Little Mountain) and follow SC 202 south for 1.7 miles to US 76. Turn right onto US 76 and travel for 0.5 mile to a left onto Wheeland Road (SR 20) at the sign for Dreher Island State Park. Follow Wheeland Road for 6.0 miles to where it ends at Macedonia Church Road. Go left here and travel for 1.3 miles to a left

Cypress trees grow freely under water.

You can camp right along the edge of Lake Murray at Dreher Island State Park.

onto Dreher Island Road. Follow this for 0.5 mile to a right onto State Park Road (SR 571) at the sign for Dreher Island Park. Travel for 2.6 miles to the entrance to the park at the end of the road.

From SC 391 (Main Street) and US 76 in Prosperity, drive south on SC 391 for 0.6 mile to where SC 391 heads right and becomes Broad Street. At this intersection, do not go right onto SC 391 south. Instead, continue to follow Main Street straight ahead, and after 0.8 mile it becomes Macedonia Church Road. Follow this road for 8.0 miles (from the junction with Broad Street) to a left onto Dreher Island Road and follow the directions above.

GPS coordinates: N34 05.748 / W81 24.915

Maps: *DeLorme: South Carolina Atlas and Gazetteer* page 35, E8

About the campground: A narrow strip of land juts out deep into Lake Murray, forming the peninsula that houses Dreher Island State Park. With 12 miles of shoreline, this perfect lakefront location is a boat enthusiast's dream! A busy boat ramp, with a tackle shop next to it, has ample parking for boat trailers. And there's even an in-water fueling station for added convenience. You can drive your boat right up to many of the campsites, or fish from the banks provided you have a South Carolina state fishing license. Licenses are available in the tackle shop, but you must pay with cash only. Although there is no designated swim beach, swimming is permitted in the park, but do so at your own risk. A few hiking trails pass through the park, and there are several gorgeous picnic shelters along the shores of Lake Murray. The campground is split into two loops at opposite ends of the park. In loop A, every campsite is paved, and many are on the water's edge, but they are right on top of each other, so you are definitely lacking privacy. Loop B has a handful of campsites dedicated for tent campers only. Although some of the sites in loop B are close together, this loop is very wooded, offering much more privacy and shade compared to loop A. Although this is a camping guidebook, I must mention the cabins/villas that this wonderful park has to offer. Each is waterfront, with a fireplace, screened porch, and its own personal boat dock. This is a great alternative for those times that foul weather drives you from your tent.

Winnsboro Area

Campground	Total sites	Hookup sites	Max. RV length	Hookups	Toilets	Showers	Drinking water	Dump station	Recreation	Fee	Reservations
45 Lake Wateree State Park	72	72	60'	E, W	F	Y	Y	Y	H, S, F, B, L, P	$$-$$$	Y

45 Lake Wateree State Park

Location: 881 State Park Rd., Winnsboro; about 12 miles northeast of Winnsboro, and about 18 miles southwest of Lancaster
Season: Year-round
Sites: 72
Maximum length: 60 feet
Facilities: Flush toilets, hot showers, electric, water, fire rings, picnic tables, dump station, ice and firewood for sale, pet friendly
Fee per night: $$-$$$
Management: South Carolina Department of Natural Resources
Contact: (803) 482-6401; www.southcarolinaparks.com/lakewateree/camping.aspx; for reservations call (866) 345-7275 or visit www.reserveamerica.com
Finding the campground: From I-77 get off at exit 41 and drive east on Durham Place Road (SR 41) for approximately 2.7 miles to a left onto US 21. Follow US 21 north for 2.0 miles to a right onto River Road (SR 101) and travel for 5.1 miles to the entrance to the park on the left.

From the junction of US 21 and SC 200 near Mitford, drive south on US 21 for 7.5 miles to a left onto River Road (SR 101) at the sign for Lake Wateree State Park and follow the directions above.
GPS coordinates: N34 25.871 / W80 52.209
Maps: *DeLorme: South Carolina Atlas and Gazetteer* page 27, G9
About the campground: Trees offer lots of shade, and just enough privacy in between campsites at Lake Wateree State Park. The lake is visible from most of the sites, and some have it as their very own backyard. A few of the sites are even wheelchair accessible. There's a boat ramp with plenty of parking for trailers, and the park office doubles as a tackle shop. An in-water fueling station makes it super convenient to stay out and play all day on the calm waters of Lake Wateree. If you don't have a boat, you can still enjoy the lake from land. There's a swimming area, and a wonderful picnic area rests right on the water's edge. You can bring your own rod and reel, or borrow one from the park since they have a great loaner program in the park's office. But before casting your line, be sure you obtain a South Carolina state fishing license. A nature trail leads out onto a peninsula on the lake before looping back to the trailhead. Mountain bikes are welcome on this trail, but I wouldn't really say that the park has mountain biking, since this trail is only 0.7 mile long. Bikes are welcome on the roads throughout the park, but again, this is a small park, so don't expect to get miles of riding in unless you head out of the park.

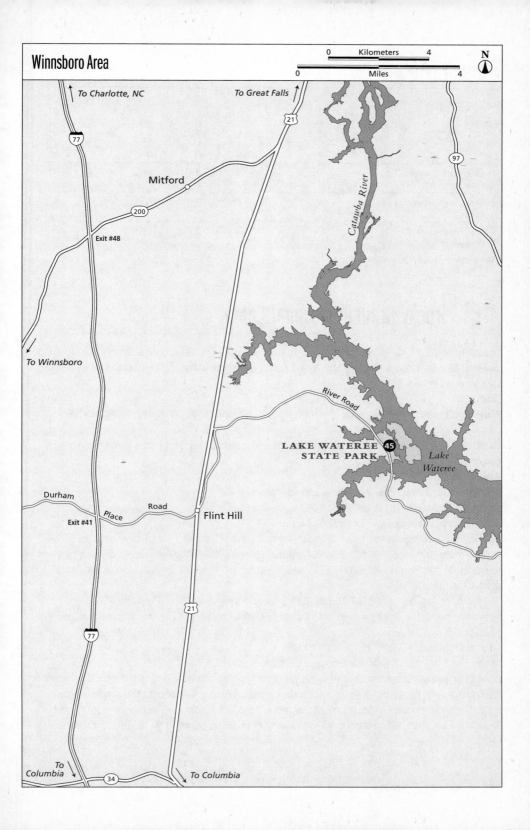

Winnsboro Area

0 — Kilometers — 4

0 — Miles — 4

N

To Charlotte, NC

To Great Falls

77

21

97

Mitford

200

Exit #48

To Winnsboro

Catawba River

River Road

LAKE WATEREE STATE PARK 45

Lake Wateree

Durham Place Road

Exit #41

Flint Hill

21

77

To Columbia

34

To Columbia

Whitmire Area

Campground	Total sites	Hookup sites	Max. RV length	Hookups	Toilets	Showers	Drinking water	Dump station	Recreation	Fee	Reservations
46 **Rocky Branch Seasonal Camp**	10	0	40'	N	V	N	N	N	H, F, B*, L*	$	N
47 **Collins Creek Seasonal Camp**	36	0	40'	N	V	Y*	Y	N	H, F*, P*	$	N
48 **Brick House Campground**	21	0	40'	N	V	N	N	N	H, M, R, O	$	N

* See campground entry for specific information

46 Rocky Branch Seasonal Camp

Location: About 17 miles west of Winnsboro, about 19 miles northeast of Newberry
Season: Mid-Sept–Jan 4 and late Mar–May 3 (exact dates change yearly; contact the forest service for more information)
Sites: 10
Maximum length: 40 feet, but there are a limited number of sites that can accommodate this size RV
Facilities: Vault toilet, hand water pump (must boil water for drinking), primitive fire rings, pet friendly
Fee per night: $
Management: Sumter National Forest–Enoree District
Contact: (803) 276-4810; (864) 427-9858; www.fs.usda.gov/recarea/scnfs/recreation/camping-cabins/recarea/?recid=47241&actid=29
Finding the campground: From I-26 near Newberry, get off at exit 74 and drive east on SC 34 for 4.3 miles to a stop sign at US 176. Continue to follow SC 34 for another 11.6 miles to a left onto Cooper Holmes Road (FR 412) and travel for 1.6 miles to the entrance to the campground on the left.

From the junction of SC 34 and SC 215 in Salem Crossroads, drive west on SC 34 for approximately 2.9 miles to a right onto Cooper Holmes Road (FR 412) and follow the directions above.
GPS coordinates: N34 26.102 / W81 19.699
Maps: *DeLorme: South Carolina Atlas and Gazetteer* page 26, G4
About the campground: Located at the southern edge of the Sumter National Forest, this small hunt camp is composed of a single loop with ten campsites nestled among the longleaf pine trees. The sites are simply flat grassy areas, and a handful of them have cement block fire rings. There's a vault toilet, a few trash cans, and a lone hand water pump in the middle of the loop.

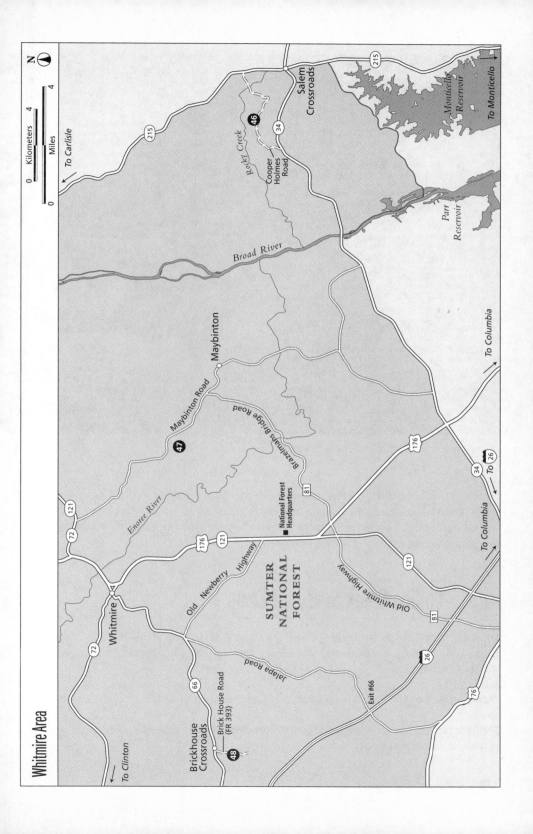

Whitmire Area

To Carlisle

215

Kilometers
0   4

Miles
0   4

N

To Clinton

72

Whitmire

66

121

72

Brickhouse
Crossroads

48

Brick House Road
(FR 393)

Jalapa Road

Old   Newberry   Highway

176

121

National Forest
Headquarters

SUMTER
NATIONAL
FOREST

Old Whitmire Highway

81

Exit #66

26

76

To Columbia

121

81

34

To 26

176

To Columbia

47

Enoree River

Maybinton Road

Maybinton

Brazelmans Bridge Road

Broad River

Parr
Reservoir

Salem
Crossroads

34

46

Cooper
Holmes Road

Rocky Creek

215

215

Monticello
Reservoir

To Monticello

These pigs seem to enjoy wallowing in the mud.

Be advised, you must boil any water from the pump prior to consumption. With the exception of the birds serenading you, the camping at Rocky Branch really doesn't offer anything special. Nearby, you'll find some hiking trails and a boat access area to the Parr Reservoir, but the area was primarily designed for and is used by hunters.

47 Collins Creek Seasonal Camp

Location: About 19 miles southeast of Union, and about 17 miles north of Newberry
Season: Mid-Sept–Jan 4 and late Mar–May 3 (exact dates change yearly; contact the forest service for more information)
Sites: 36
Maximum length: 40 feet, but there are a limited number of sites that can accommodate this size RV
Facilities: Vault toilets, water spigots dispersed, hot outdoor shower, occasional primitive fire rings, occasional lantern holders, pet friendly

Fee per night: $

Management: Sumter National Forest–Enoree District

Contact: (803) 276-4810; (864) 427-9858; www.fs.usda.gov/recarea/scnfs/recreation/camping-cabins/recarea/?recid=47237&actid=29

Finding the campground: From the junction of SC 72 and US 176 in Whitmire, drive east on SC 72 for 1.1 miles to a right onto Maybinton Road (SR 45) and travel for 4.4 miles to a right onto FR 393. Follow FR 393 for 0.3 mile to the campground on the left.

From the junction of SC 34 and SC 215 in Salem Crossroads, drive west on SC 34 for approximately 8.1 miles to a right onto Mt. Pleasant Road (SR 28). Travel for 3.7 miles to a hard right onto Maybinton Road. Follow Maybinton Road for 8.0 miles to a left onto FR 393 and follow the directions above.

GPS coordinates: N34 28.327 / W81 31.472

Maps: *DeLorme: South Carolina Atlas and Gazetteer* page 26, F2

About the campground: Much nicer than its fellow forest service seasonal camp Rocky Branch, the campground at Collins Creek is nicely wooded, and the sites are slightly spread out. This busy hunt camp has flat campsites with barely anything on them. A few have lantern holders, while others have primitive fire rings. The Jews Harp Spring Trailhead is at the south end of the campground and leads to a natural spring with a unique carving in it. This 0.7-mile trail is open to hikers only. Aside from hiking and hunting, other recreational activities include picnicking and fishing at the nearby Molly's Rock Picnic area. But you must have a South Carolina state fishing license before you bait your hook.

48 Brick House Campground

Location: About 5 miles east of Clinton, and about 7 miles southwest of Whitmire

Season: Year-round

Sites: 21

Maximum length: 40 feet

Facilities: Vault toilets, NO water, fire rings, picnic tables, lantern holders, some sites have charcoal grills, pet friendly

Fee per night: $

Management: Sumter National Forest–Enoree District

Contact: (803) 276-4810; (864) 427-9858; www.fs.usda.gov/recarea/scnfs/recreation/camping-cabins/recarea/?recid=47233&actid=29

Finding the campground: From I-26 get off at exit 60 and drive east on SC 66 (Whitmire Highway) and travel for approximately 3.6 miles to a right onto Brick House Road (FR 358). Travel for 0.4 mile to the campground on your right.

From the junction of SC 66 and SC 72 in Whitmire, drive west on SC 66 for 7.5 miles to a left onto Brick House Road (FR 358) and follow the directions above.

GPS coordinates: N34 26.875 / W81 42.355

Maps: *DeLorme: South Carolina Atlas and Gazetteer* page 25, G9

About the campground: Brick House is easily the nicest national forest campground in the Enoree Ranger District. The sites are well groomed and spaced out just enough to give you a dash of privacy. Horse campers are welcome, and there are designated areas on the outskirts of

Prevent forest fires—be sure your campfire is completely out before leaving your campsite.

each campsite where you can tether your trusty steed. The Buncombe Horse Trailhead is just 0.25 mile away, and there's ample parking for your horse trailer, making this nearly a "ride-in ride-out" campground. This 30-plus-mile trail traverses the Sumter National Forest, and is open to hikers and mountain bikers as well. The Enoree off-highway vehicle (OHV) trail system is also within easy reach, making this an ideal location for all your outdoor explorations. Here, and anywhere in the forest, be sure to do your part to prevent forest fires. Use caution when building your fire, never cut live trees to burn, and always make sure your fire is completely out before leaving your campsite.

Union Area

Campground	Total sites	Hookup sites	Max. RV length	Hookups	Toilets	Showers	Drinking water	Dump station	Recreation	Fee	Reservations
49 **Sedalia Campground**	12	0	40'	N	V	N	Y	N	H, F*, B*	$	N

* See campground entry for specific information

49 Sedalia Campground

Location: About 10 miles southwest of Union, and about 20 miles northeast of Laurens
Season: A limited number of sites are open year-round, and the entire campground is open from mid-Sept–Jan 4 and late Mar–May 3 (exact dates change yearly; contact the forest service for more information)
Sites: 9; 3 group camp areas are also available and can accommodate up to 30 people each
Maximum length: 40 feet
Facilities: Vault toilets, water spigots dispersed, primitive rock fire rings, pet friendly
Fee per night: $

Cows are a common sight in the Piedmont.

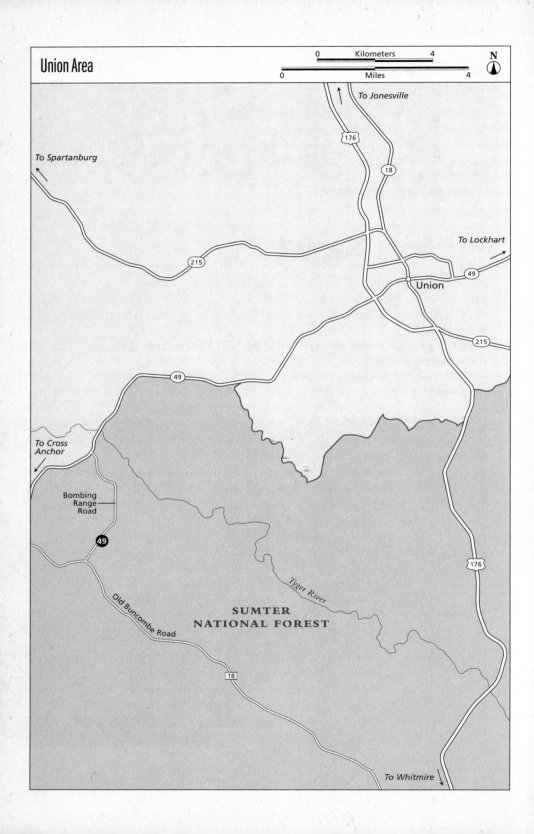

Management: Sumter National Forest–Enoree District

Contact: (803) 276-4810; (864) 427-9858; www.fs.usda.gov/recarea/scnfs/recreation/camping-cabins/recarea/?recid=47243&actid=29

Finding the campground: From the junction of SC 49 and US 176 in Union, drive west on SC 49 for 7.9 miles to a left onto Bombing Range Road (SR 481). Follow Bombing Range Road for 2.2 miles to the campground on the left.

From the junction of SC 49 and SC 56 in Cross Anchor, drive east on SC 49 for 7.8 miles to a right onto Bombing Range Road (SR 481) and follow the directions above.

GPS coordinates: N34 37.848 / W81 44.318

Maps: *DeLorme: South Carolina Atlas and Gazetteer* page 25, C9

About the campground: The Enoree District of the Sumter National Forest dropped the ball here. The campsites at Sedalia are stripped down to nothing but a primitive fire ring made up of rocks, and that is all. Small patches of grass laid out far too close to one another and a vault toilet are what to expect. The only water spigot I saw on my visit was in the group camping area. The upside at Sedalia is that the Palmetto Trailhead shares the property, so at least you have easy access to explore the forest around you. The Tyger River is very close, so you can go fish, as long as you carry a South Carolina state fishing license. Two state historic sites are nearby. To the east is the Rose Hill Plantation, and to the west is the Musgrove Mill, and both make a nice side trip while you're in the area.

Union to Chester Area

Campground	Total sites	Hookup sites	Max. RV length	Hookups	Toilets	Showers	Drinking water	Dump station	Recreation	Fee	Reservations
50 **Woods Ferry Campground**	26	0	35'	N	F	Y	Y	N	H, R, F, B*, L*, P	$-$$	N
51 **Chester State Park**	29	25	36'	E, W	F	Y	Y	Y	H, F, B*, L*, DG, P	$$	Y

* See campground entry for specific information

50 Woods Ferry Campground

Location: About 18 miles east of Union and about 14 miles west of Chester
Season: Apr 1–Oct 31
Sites: 25; 1 group camp area is also available and can accommodate up to 15 people
Maximum length: 35 feet
Facilities: Flush toilets, hot showers, water spigots dispersed, fire rings, picnic tables, some lantern holders, pet friendly
Fee per night: $-$$
Management: Sumter National Forest–Enoree District
Contact: (803) 276-4810 or (864) 427-9858; www.fs.usda.gov/recarea/scnfs/recreation/camping-cabins/recarea/?recid=47245&actid=29
Finding the campground: From the junction of SC 9 and US 321 North in Chester, drive west on SC 9 for 9.4 miles to a left onto Roy Wade Road (SR 535) at the sign for Woods Ferry Recreation Area. Travel for 0.4 mile to a left onto Woods Ferry Road (SR 49). Follow Woods Ferry Road for 2.0 miles to a right onto Buck's Grave Road. Travel for 3.1 miles to where the road ends at Park Road. Go right, and drive for 1.3 miles to where the road ends at the campground.

From the junction of SC 9 and SC 49 North in Lockhart, drive east on SC 9 for 4.3 miles to a right onto Woods Ferry Road (SR 49). Travel for 2.3 miles to a right onto Buck's Grave Road and follow the directions above.
GPS coordinates: N34 41.979 / W81 27.058
Maps: *DeLorme: South Carolina Atlas and Gazetteer* page 26, B2
About the campground: Topography at last. Not only does the campground sit within a hilly portion of the Enoree District of the Sumter National Forest, but the sites are wooded and spaced well apart from one another, offering campers lots of privacy. Nearly half of the campsites have horse corrals on them, and several others have designated areas on the outskirts of the loop where you can tether your horse. But please do not tether your horse directly to the trees. Instead, hang a high line and hitch your horse to that. The Woods Ferry Horse Trail system can be accessed right from the property, making this a ride-in/ride-out locale. An intimate picnic area with tree-lined paths lies between the campground and the Broad River, giving campers a wonderful place to picnic. You can fish from the banks, provided you have your South Carolina state fishing license, or launch a canoe or kayak and

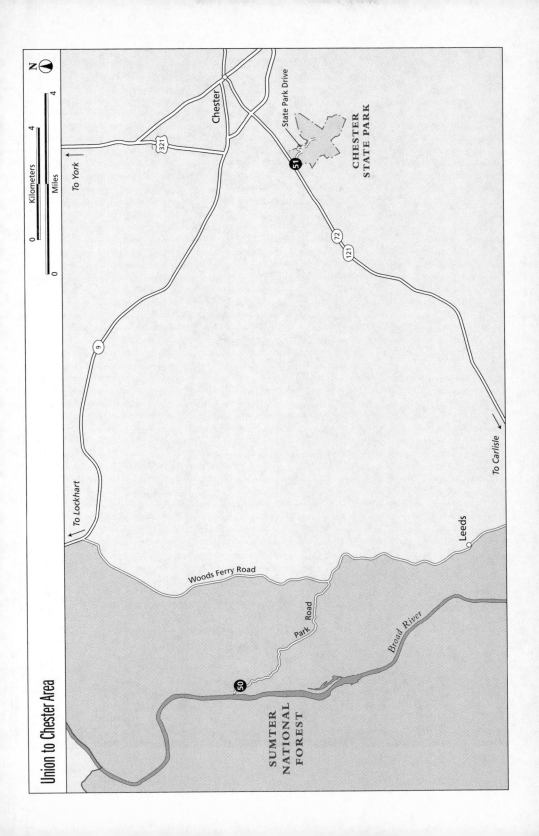

Union to Chester Area

N

0   4   Kilometers

0   4   Miles

Chester

321

To York

State Park Drive

51

CHESTER
STATE PARK

72

121

9

To Lockhart

To Carlisle

Woods Ferry Road

Park   Road

Leeds

50

Broad River

SUMTER
NATIONAL
FOREST

Palmetto Pride waves in the wind below Old Glory.

enjoy a day out on the river. With a steady breeze blowing off the river's edge, and an area rich in history, Woods Ferry gets a thumbs up from me. The only drawback is that there's a rifle range right down the road, so the sound of gunshots in the distance is not uncommon.

51 Chester State Park

Location: 759 State Park Dr., Chester; about 2 miles southwest of Chester
Season: Year-round
Sites: 25; 4 group camp areas are also available and can accommodate up to 50 people
Maximum length: 40 feet, but there are a limited number of sites that can accommodate this size RV
Facilities: Flush toilets, hot showers, electric, water, fire rings, picnic tables, dump station, firewood for sale, pet friendly
Fee per night: $$
Management: South Carolina Department of Natural Resources
Contact: (803) 385-2680; www.southcarolinaparks.com/chester/camping.aspx; for reservations call (866) 345-7275 or visit www.reserveamerica.com

Chester State Park has the perfect place for a family gathering

Finding the campground: From the junction of SC 72 and US 321, drive south on SC 72 for 1.4 miles to a left onto State Park Drive at the entrance to the park.

From the junction of SC 72 and SC 215 near Carlisle, drive north on SC 72 for 11.0 miles to a right onto State Park Drive at the entrance to the park.

GPS coordinates: N34 40.994 / W81 14.922

Maps: *DeLorme: South Carolina Atlas and Gazetteer* page 26, C5

About the campground: The day-use area at Chester State Park is actually nicer than the campground. With picnic shelters overlooking the lake, a boathouse with rentals, a fishing pier, nature trail, and open fields to play a game of kickball or toss a Frisbee, there's plenty to do. A boat ramp is also available, but no gas motors are allowed on the lake. Most of the park was built by the Civilian Conservation Corps back in the 1930s, but there's also a newly designed disc golf course on the property. The park sits just outside the town of Chester, and while you may enjoy your space on weekdays, this lakeside loop fills up quickly on the weekends. A few sites overlook the lake, and a small fishing pier is dedicated for campers only, but you must obtain a South Carolina state fishing license prior to casting your line.

Rock Hill Area

Campground	Total sites	Hookup sites	Max. RV length	Hookups	Toilets	Showers	Drinking water	Dump station	Recreation	Fee	Reservations
52 **Andrew Jackson State Park**	26	25	38'	E, W	F	Y	Y	Y	H, F, B*, L*, HS, P	$$	Y
53 **Anne Springs Close Greenway Primitive Campground**	12	0	n/a	N	F	Y	Y	N	H, M, R, F*, B*, L*, P	$-$$$	Y*
54 **Ebenezer County Park**	71	71	None	E, W, S	F	Y	Y	Y	S, F, B, L, BB, HS, V, P	$$-$$$	Y*

* See campground entry for specific information

52 Andrew Jackson State Park

Location: 196 Andrew Jackson Park Rd., Lancaster; about 9 miles north of Lancaster and 12 miles southeast of Rock Hill
Season: Year-round
Sites: 25; 1 group camp area is also available and can accommodate up to 50 people
Maximum length: 38 feet
Facilities: Flush toilets, hot showers, electric, water, fire rings, picnic tables, dump station, pet friendly
Fee per night: $$
Management: South Carolina Department of Natural Resources
Contact: (803) 285-3344; www.southcarolinaparks.com/andrewjackson/camping.aspx; for reservations call (866) 345-7275 or visit www.reserveamerica.com
Finding the campground: From the junction of US 521 and SC 5 near Rock Hill, drive north on US 521 for 0.5 mile to the entrance to the park on your right.
From the junction of US 521 and SC 75 West, drive south on US 521 for 1.5 miles to the entrance to the park on the left.
GPS coordinates: N34 50.583 / W80 48.575
Maps: *DeLorme: South Carolina Atlas and Gazetteer* page 21, H10
About the campground: Within this historically named park, a single, small loop comprises the campground. Most of the campsites are within view of the park's lake, but they are not very private, and only a handful rest upon her shores. A few of the sites are wheelchair accessible as is the petite fishing pier that extends out into the lake. Boat rentals are available for a reasonable fee ($-$$), or you can cart your own nonmotorized boat to the boat launch. Fishing is permitted from the pier, banks, or boat, but you must obtain a South Carolina state fishing license prior to breaking out your rod and reel. A pair of picnic shelters is quite charming, and two nature trails give you the chance to explore this 360-acre park by land. A historical one-room schoolhouse and an on-site museum are open on the weekends, or by appointment during the week. Both give visitors a bit of history and insight about the Revolutionary War and of the park's namesake, President Andrew Jackson.

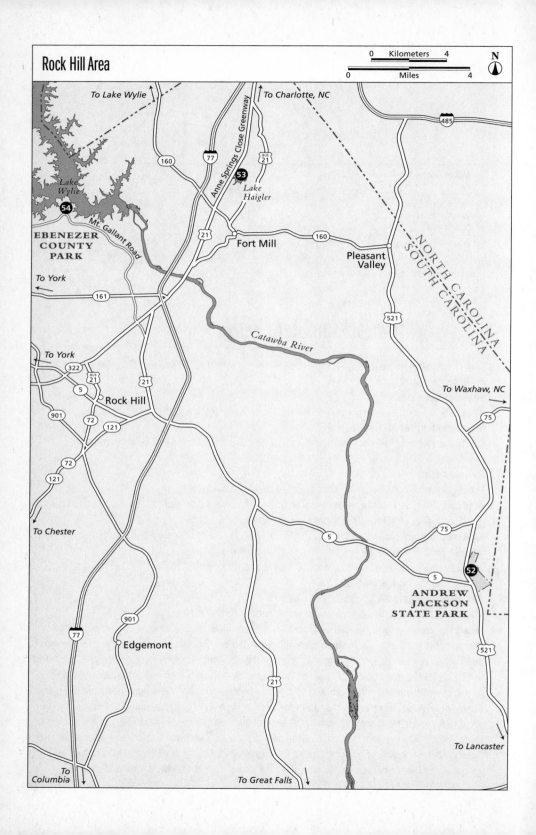

Rock Hill Area

Kilometers 0 — 4
Miles 0 — 4

N

To Lake Wylie

To Charlotte, NC

485

160

77

BUS 21

Anne Springs Close Greenway

53

Lake Haigler

Lake Wylie

54

EBENEZER COUNTY PARK

Mt. Gallant Road

21

Fort Mill

160

Pleasant Valley

NORTH CAROLINA
SOUTH CAROLINA

To York

161

521

Catawba River

To York

322

BUS 21

5

21

To Waxhaw, NC

75

Rock Hill

901

72

121

72

121

5

75

To Chester

52

ANDREW JACKSON STATE PARK

5

77

901

Edgemont

521

21

To Columbia

To Great Falls

To Lancaster

53 Anne Springs Close Greenway Primitive Campground

Location: About 3 miles northeast of Rock Hill and about 14 miles southwest of Charlotte, North Carolina
Season: Year-round
Sites: 12
Maximum length: n/a
Facilities: Flush toilets, hot showers, no water, primitive fire rings, fish cleaning tables, pet friendly
Fee per night: $-$$$
Management: Leroy Springs and Company
Contact: (803) 548-7252; www.leroysprings.com/default.asp?lsc=260
Finding the campground: From the junction of US 21 Bypass and SC 160 near Fort Mill, drive north on US 21 Bypass for 1.6 miles to the entrance to the greenway on the right.

From the junction of US 21 Bypass and SC 460 (Springfield Parkway), drive north on US 21 Bypass for 1.2 miles to the entrance to the greenway on the left.
GPS coordinates: N35 02.150 / W80 56.525
Maps: *DeLorme: South Carolina Atlas and Gazetteer* page 21, E9
About the campground: What an amazing piece of property the Anne Springs Close Greenway has assembled! Over 40 miles of hiking, mountain bike, and bridle trails crisscross throughout this 2,100-acre plot of land. With paddocks and ponds, canoe and kayak rentals, geocaching, guided hikes, and historical buildings to tour, the people of Fort Mill are fortunate to have such a wonderful resource within their reach. The lakes and ponds are stocked with fish, but you must be a Greenway member to fish here. You can rent a canoe or kayak and paddle about on Lake Haigler, or launch your own nonmotorized boat at any one of the three boat ramps on the property. The camping is primitive and requires a short walk of less than 0.1 mile up to 0.5 mile to reach the sites. A dozen campsites, each with a table and a stone fire ring, sit scattered about in the woods along the northern banks of Lake Haigler. There is a bathhouse near the parking area, with flush toilets and hot showers, but there are no water spigots and no potable water in the camping area, so be sure to bring plenty along with you. You must be at least 21 years of age to reserve a campsite, and the maximum stay is 1 week.

The Greenway also offers horse camping, with paddocks for you to house your horse. But be aware, there is not much in the way of shade in the horse camping area. Contact the Greenway directly, or check out their website for trail maps and further information.

54 Ebenezer County Park

Location: 4490 Boatshore Rd., Rock Hill; on the southern edge of Lake Wylie, about 15 miles southwest of Charlotte, North Carolina
Season: Year-round
Sites: 71
Maximum length: None
Facilities: Flush toilets, hot showers, electric, water, fire rings, picnic tables, dump station, pet friendly
Fee per night: $$–$$$
Management: York County Parks and Recreation
Contact: (803) 366-6620; www.yorkcountygov.com/ebenezer
Finding the campground: From the junction of SC 274 and SC 55 near Lake Wylie, drive south on SC 274 for 5.9 miles to a left onto Mt. Gallant Road (SR 195) at the sign for Ebenezer Park. Travel for 3.5 miles to a left onto Boatshore Road. Follow Boatshore Road for 0.3 mile to the entrance to the park.

From the junction of SC 274 and SC 161 in Newport, drive north on SC 274 for approximately 1.3 miles to a right onto Mt. Gallant Road (SR 195) and follow the directions above.

From I-77 in Rock Hill, get off at exit 82 and drive west on SC 161 for approximately 0.9 mile to a right onto Mt. Gallant Road (SR 195). Follow Mt. Gallant Road for 4.1 miles to a right onto Boatshore Road. Travel for 0.3 mile to the entrance to the park.
GPS coordinates: N35 01.334 / W81 02.581
Maps: *DeLorme: South Carolina Atlas and Gazetteer* page 21, E7
About the campground: This busy county park is obviously more about the location than it is about the camping experience. Resting along the southern shores of Lake Wylie, Ebenezer has a prime waterfront location. The park has a boat ramp that's full of activity but does provide a decent amount of parking for boat trailers. There's a swim beach, volleyball and basketball nets, and they even have a horseshoe pit. You can fish from the banks in certain areas of the park, but you must obtain a South Carolina state fishing license before you unpack your pole. The campground is composed of 71 sites that are split up into a few different areas within the park. Sites 1–30 are basically wide open, and right on top of each other, but they do have the perk of having a lakefront view. The remaining 41 campsites sit in an area that is wooded, but the sites are still right on top of each other. Another drawback is that this part of the campground backs up to a neighborhood, so the back boundary of your campsite is a chain-link fence line. The Catawba River, named for the Catawba Indians, forms and flows through Lake Wylie. You may enjoy a quick jaunt over to the town of Rock Hill to visit the Catawba Cultural Center. The center has exhibits, a nature trail, and historic archives of the many traditions of the Catawba Native American tribe. It's also home to South Carolina's largest annual Native American gathering. At the time of this writing in late 2013, the park was working on implementing a reservation system, so check with them directly for further information.

Blacksburg Area

Campground	Total sites	Hookup sites	Max. RV length	Hookups	Toilets	Showers	Drinking water	Dump station	Recreation	Fee	Reservations
55 **Kings Mountain State Park**	143	115	45'	E, W	F	Y	Y	Y	H, R, F, B*, BB, DG, V, P, **	$$	Y

* See campground entry for specific information

55 Kings Mountain State Park

Location: 1277 Park Rd., Blacksburg; about 14 miles northwest of York, and about 7 miles south of Kings Mountain, North Carolina
Season: Year-round
Sites: 125; 15 equestrian campsites are also available; 1 primitive group camping area is also available and can accommodate up to 30 people; 1 youth group camp, Camp Cherokee; 1 group camp open to all groups, Camp York

Come and sit a spell at Kings Mountain State Park.

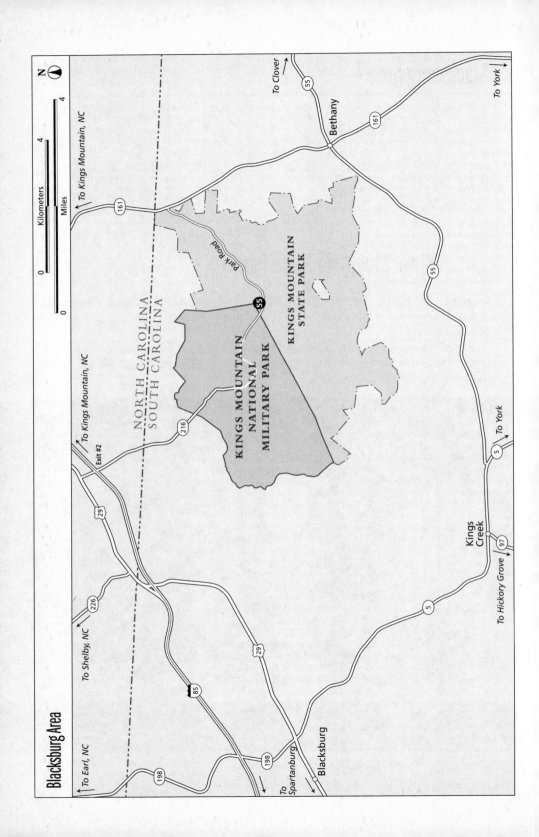

Blacksburg Area

To Earl, NC

To Shelby, NC

198

226

29

85

To Spartanburg

198

Blacksburg

29

5

Kings Creek

97

To Hickory Grove

5

To York

Exit #2

To Kings Mountain, NC

216

NORTH CAROLINA
SOUTH CAROLINA

**KINGS MOUNTAIN
NATIONAL
MILITARY PARK**

Park Road

55

**KINGS MOUNTAIN
STATE PARK**

55

To Kings Mountain, NC

161

161

Bethany

55

To Clover

To York

N

Kilometers

0   4

Miles

0   4

Airstream campers are an American classic.

Maximum Length: 45 feet, but there are a limited number of sites that can accommodate this size RV

Facilities: Flush toilets, hot showers, electric, water, fire rings, picnic tables, dump station, ice and firewood for sale, pet friendly

Fee per night: $$

Management: South Carolina Department of Natural Resources

Contact: (803) 222-3209; www.southcarolinaparks.com/kingsmountain/camping.aspx; for reservations call (866) 345-7275 or visit www.reserveamerica.com; for equestrian camping reservations, contact the park directly at (803) 222-3209

Finding the campground: From I-85 in North Carolina, and get off at NC exit 2 and drive south on Highway 216/Park Road for 4.9 miles to the entrance to the park.

From the junction of SC 161 and SC 55 in Bethany, drive north on SC 161 for 3.2 miles to a left onto Park Road. Follow Park Road for 0.7 mile to the entrance to the park. Note: As you travel on Park Road, you will pass through Kings Mountain National Military Park.

GPS coordinates: N35 08.098 / W81 21.539

Maps: *DeLorme: South Carolina Atlas and Gazetteer* page 20, C4

About the campground: Rich in history, the park butts up to Kings Mountain National Military Park to the west, and borders North Carolina to the north. An actual living farm greets you just inside the park, and mimics what life in South Carolina was like in the early 1800s. The park covers nearly 7,000 acres and uses most of it. But due to this large size, you may find that it's a bit poorly marked. Two lakes can be found at opposite ends of the park, and you are welcome to fish from the banks of Lake Crawford, or by boat on the larger Lake York, provided that you have a South Carolina state fishing license. Boat rentals are available, or you can launch your own canoe or kayak for a nominal fee ($). Hiking and bridle trails loop around the park and even connect to the military park next door. One hiking trail is an out-and-back-style trail and leads all the way up to Crowders Mountain State Park in North Carolina. Giant, spread-out loops comprise the campground, but surprisingly, clusters of campsites tend to be a bit overcrowded in this heavily wooded park. You are not at a loss for things to do. Along with the lakes and trails, the park has a volleyball and basketball net, a full disc golf course, and oddly enough, a ping-pong table. A primitive equestrian camping area is also available, with fifteen campsites, a central water spigot, and a vault toilet. Two unique group camps, Camp Cherokee and Camp York, can also be found within Kings Mountain State Park.

Spartanburg Area

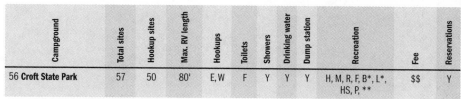

Campground	Total sites	Hookup sites	Max. RV length	Hookups	Toilets	Showers	Drinking water	Dump station	Recreation	Fee	Reservations
56 **Croft State Park**	57	50	80'	E, W	F	Y	Y	Y	H, M, R, F, B*, L*, HS, P, **	$$	Y

* See campground entry for specific information

56 Croft State Park

Location: 450 Croft State Park Rd., Spartanburg; about 4 miles southeast of Spartanburg
Season: Year-round
Sites: 50; 7 primitive tent sites can be rented by individuals but can also accommodate larger groups of up to 100 people
Maximum length: 80 feet
Facilities: Flush toilets, hot showers, electric, water, fire rings, picnic tables, dump station, ice and firewood for sale, pet friendly
Fee per night: $$
Management: South Carolina Department of Natural Resources
Contact: (864) 585-1283; www.southcarolinaparks.com/croft/camping.aspx; for reservations call (866) 345-7275 or visit www.reserveamerica.com
Finding the campground: From the junction of SC 56 and SC 295 in Spartanburg, drive south on SC 56 for 2.2 miles to a left onto Dairy Ridge Road at the sign for Croft State Park. Travel for 0.3 mile to a right onto Croft State Park Road at the entrance to the park.
From the junction of SC 56 and SC 215 near Pauline, drive north on SC 56 for approximately 3.5 miles to a right onto Dairy Ridge Road and follow the directions above.
GPS coordinates: N34 53.457 / W81 52.276
Maps: *DeLorme: South Carolina Atlas and Gazetteer* page 19, G8
About the campground: Any outdoor enthusiast will certainly enjoy this heavily wooded park. Steeped in history, homesteads once stood deep in the forest surrounding the park. Then, during World War II, the area was known as Camp Croft, an army infantry training camp. Today, Croft State Park is home to 20 miles of bridle trails, 15 miles of mountain bike trails, and 2.5 miles of hiking trails. You can spend an entire day exploring the far reaches of this spacious state park, or simply sit and enjoy the pleasures of one of many picnic shelters. In the middle of the park lies Lake Craig. Boat rentals are available, or you can launch your own boat, but the lake is limited to canoes, kayaks, rowboats, or boats with electric trolling motors. You can fish from the banks or your boat, but you must obtain a South Carolina state fishing license before you break out the bait. The main attraction of Croft State Park is the equestrian features in the day-use area. The park has amazingly clean horse stables, hitching posts, plenty of parking for

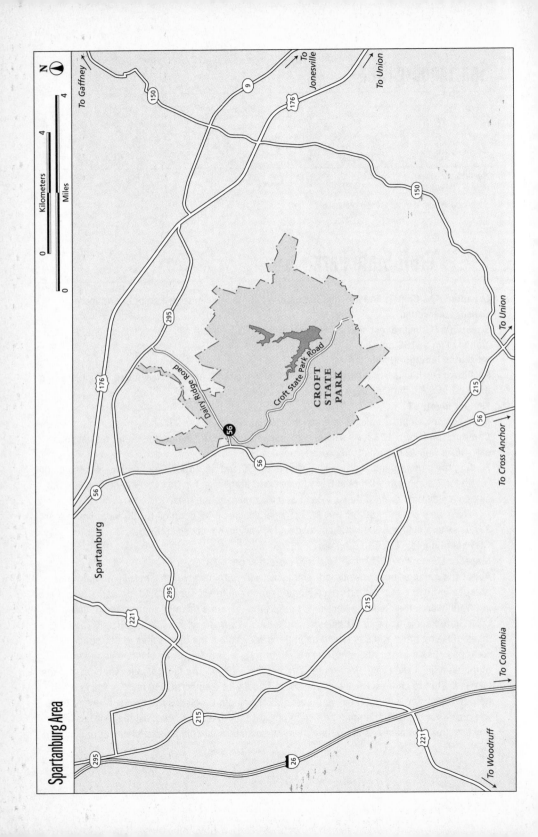

Spartanburg Area

This beautiful pinto was a bit camera shy.

trailers, and a flawless show ring. Stalls can be rented out for an additional fee ($-$$), and you must show proof of a negative Coggins test for your equine friend. Equestrian events are held monthly, and as is fitting, a horseshoe pit can also be found in the day-use area. Don't be surprised if you hear gunshots in the distance; a state shooting range sits near the south end of the park boundary.

Upcountry—
Mountains

Mountains, oh the mountains, peering back at you from afar. View after glorious view waits to greet you in the upcountry of South Carolina. Stars paint the sky as you gaze up at them from the comfort of your campsite. Sitting in the northwest corner of the state and bordered by Georgia and North Carolina, the Upcountry covers the smallest ground of any region in the state. Yet, surprisingly, it has a whopping thity-seven campgrounds or primitive campsites to boast about. With waterfalls galore and

White-tail deer are abundant in the South Carolina Upcountry.

Upcountry-Overview

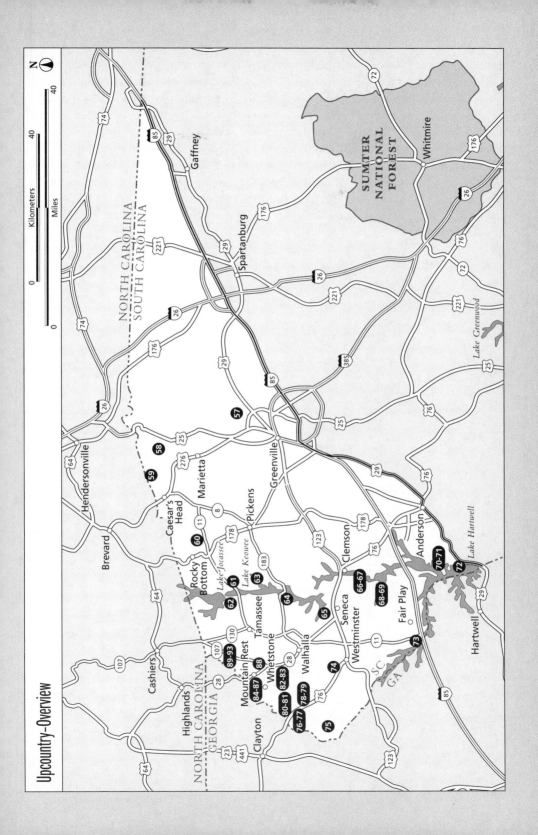

pristine mountain lakes, you'll be mesmerized by the beauty before you. Camp by a river as it rushes by, or be awestruck by the crisp green water of Lake Jocassee and Lake Keowee. Water-ski on a lake surrounded by mountains, or tickle the water as you try your hand at fly fishing. Climb to the top of Table Rock, or delve inside the Stumphouse Tunnel. Hike on the famous Foothills Trail, or mountain bike at Paris Mountain State Park. Visit the Cowpens National Battlefield in Gaffney, or go antiquing in the historic settlement towns of Westminster and Walhalla. The possibilities are endless. Whatever your pleasure, you're sure to find it here, in the magnificent Upcountry of South Carolina. *Falcon Guides: Hiking Waterfalls in Georgia and South Carolina* is a great guide and a valuable tool to help you find the many waterfalls within the region.

Greenville Area

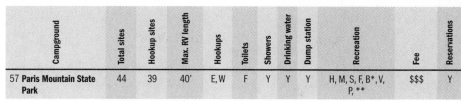

Campground	Total sites	Hookup sites	Max. RV length	Hookups	Toilets	Showers	Drinking water	Dump station	Recreation	Fee	Reservations
57 **Paris Mountain State Park**	44	39	40'	E, W	F	Y	Y	Y	H, M, S, F, B*, V, P, **	$$$	Y

* See campground entry for specific information

57 Paris Mountain State Park

Location: 2401 State Park Rd., Greenville; about 2 miles north of Greenville
Season: Year-round
Sites: 39; 5 backcountry campsites are also available
Maximum length: 40 feet
Facilities: Flush toilets, hot showers, electric, water, fire rings, picnic tables, dump station, pet friendly
Fee per night: $$$
Management: South Carolina Department of Natural Resources
Contact: (864) 244-5565; www.southcarolinaparks.com/parismountain/camping.aspx; for reservations call (866) 345-7275 or visit www.reserveamerica.com
Finding the campground: From the junction of SC 253 and SC 290 in Sandy Flat, drive southwest on SC 253 for 2.9 miles to a hard right onto State Park Road (SR 344) at the sign for Paris Mountain State Park. Travel for 0.8 mile to the entrance to the park on the left.
From the junction of SC 253 and US 25 in Greenville, drive northeast on SC 253 for approximately 2.1 miles to a left onto State Park Road (SR 344) at the sign for Paris Mountain State Park and follow the directions above.
GPS coordinates: N34 55.527 / W82 21.927
Maps: *DeLorme: South Carolina Atlas and Gazetteer* page 18, F1
About the campground: What a terrific park! With subtle, hilly topography, and a lakeside picnic area, this wonderful state park makes a great retreat on any day of the week. There's something for everyone at Paris Mountain. Hiking and mountain bike trails traverse the undulating, wooded terrain. There's a volleyball net, open fields to play in, and a baseball field. The lake has a swim area and a floating dock, or you can fish from the banks as long as you acquire your South Carolina state fishing license. The park rents canoes, kayaks, and pedal boats, but no personal boats are permitted in the park. The campground sits atop a wooded hill, and the loop has two distinct sections. One section of the loop has deeper, flat, level pavement, making it convenient for RV campers. The other part of the loop has tent pads, and is designed with tent campers in mind. Every site in the campground has its own water and electric hookups, even the tent sites, but if you are looking for a more primitive experience, the park has 5 trailside backcountry campsites as well.

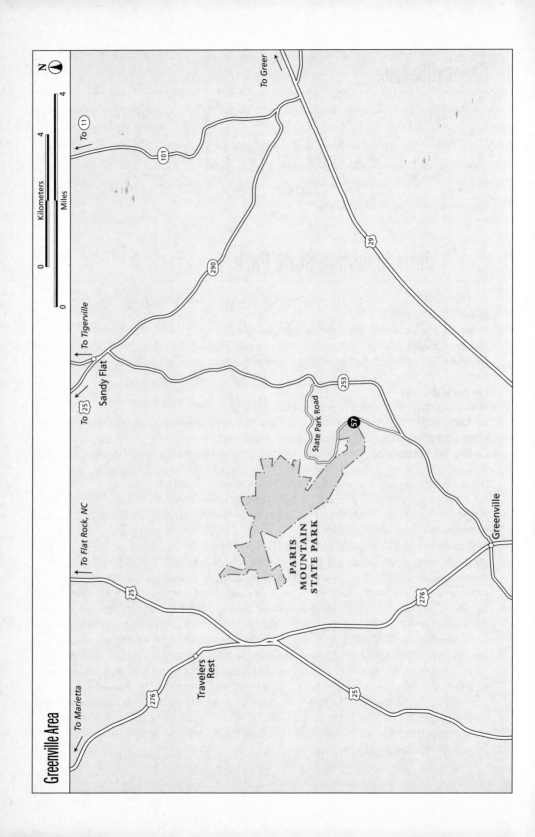

Greenville Area

Paris Mountain State Park

To Marietta

276

25

To Flat Rock, NC

25

Travelers Rest

276

PARIS
MOUNTAIN
STATE PARK

Greenville

276

25

To Tigerville

To 25

Sandy Flat

253

State Park Road

57

290

To 11

101

29

To Greer

N

Kilometers
0   4

Miles
0   4

Pickens Area

Campground	Total sites	Hookup sites	Max. RV length	Hookups	Toilets	Showers	Drinking water	Dump station	Recreation	Fee	Reservations
58 Pleasant Ridge County Park	25	25	40'	E, W	F	Y	Y	Y	H, BB, P	$$-$$$	N
59 Jones Gap State Park: Backcountry Camping	20	0	n/a	N	F	Y*	Y	N	·	H, F, P	$-$$	Y
60 Table Rock State Park	99	96	45'	E, W	F	Y	Y	Y	H, S*, F, B, L, P	$$-$$$	Y

* See campground entry for specific information

58 Pleasant Ridge County Park

Location: 4232 Hwy. 11, Marietta; about 15 miles north of Greenville
Season: Mar 1–Oct 31
Sites: 25
Maximum length: 40 feet
Facilities: Flush toilets, hot showers, electric, water, fire rings, picnic tables, dump station, firewood for sale at times, pet friendly
Fee per night: $$-$$$
Management: Greenville County Parks and Recreation Commission
Contact: (864) 288-6470; www.greenvillerec.com/parks/pleasant-ridge
Finding the campground: From the junction of SC 11 and US 25 in Lima, drive west on SC 11 for 2.0 miles to a right onto SC 187 at the entrance to the park.
   From the junction of US 276 and SC 11 near Cleveland, drive east on SC 11 for approximately 2.5 miles to a left onto SC 187 at the entrance to the park.
GPS coordinates: N35 05.098 / W82 28.690
Maps: *DeLorme: South Carolina Atlas and Gazetteer* page 17, D10
About the campground: This small community park has an open field with a limited playground, a nature trail, and a tiny creek running through it. The creek and the history of the park are certainly the highlight. Pleasant Ridge was home to the first African-American park superintendent in the state of South Carolina, Leroy Smith, who held the position for twenty-eight years until his death in 1979. As for the campground, it has all the typical amenities and even offers water and electric on every site. But the sites are not very private, and you can hear the steady flow of traffic passing by on SC 11.

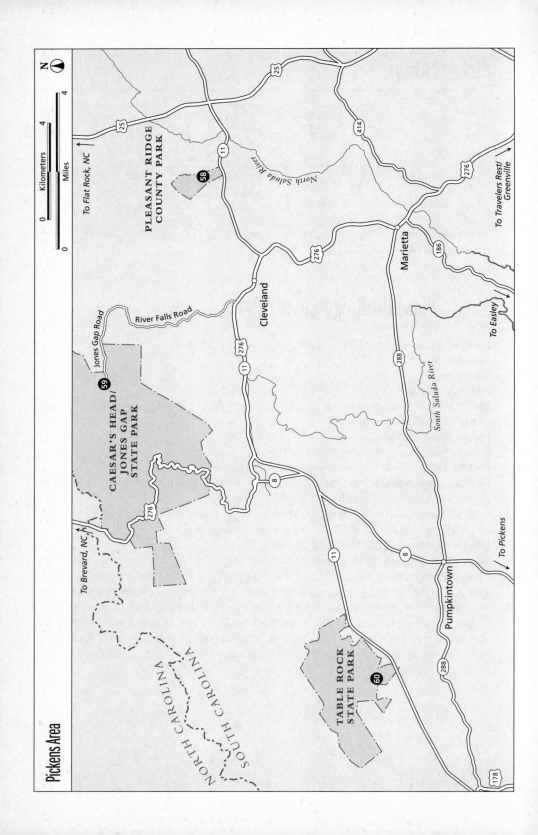

Pickens Area

N

0 4 Kilometers
0 4 Miles

To Flat Rock, NC

25

25

11

58

PLEASANT RIDGE
COUNTY PARK

North Saluda River

414

276

276

Marietta

186

To Travelers Rest/
Greenville

To Easley

Cleveland

11

276

River Falls Road

Jones Gap Road

59

CAESAR'S HEAD/
JONES GAP
STATE PARK

276

To Brevard, NC

8

288

South Saluda River

NORTH CAROLINA

SOUTH CAROLINA

11

TABLE ROCK
STATE PARK

60

8

288

Pumpkintown

To Pickens

178

59 Jones Gap State Park: Backcountry Camping

Location: 303 Jones Gap Rd., Marietta; about 25 miles northwest of Greenville
Season: Year-round
Sites: 18; 2 group camp areas are also available and can accommodate up to 20 people each
Maximum length: n/a
Facilities: Flush toilets, hot showers (available at night only), water spigot in day-use area, primitive fire rings, firewood for sale, pet friendly
Fee per night: $–$$
Management: South Carolina Department of Natural Resources
Contact: (864) 836-3647; www.southcarolinaparks.com/jonesgap/camping.aspx; for reservations call (866) 345-7275
Finding the campground: From the junction of US 276 and SC 11 East near Cleveland, drive north on US 276 for approximately 1.5 miles to a right onto River Falls Road. Follow River Falls Road for approximately 4.0 miles to a left onto Jones Gap Road and travel for approximately 1.9 miles to the entrance to the park at the end of the road.

From the junction of US 276 and SC 11 West, near Caesar's Head, drive south on US 276 for approximately 4.0 miles to a left onto River Falls Road and follow the directions above.

A hawk shows off her impressive wingspan.

GPS coordinates: N35 07.526 / W82 34.486
Maps: *DeLorme: South Carolina Atlas and Gazetteer* page 17, C9
About the campground: Trailside camping at its best! As you sit peacefully by the campfire, the crystal-clear water of the Middle Saluda River rushes by, and the constant sound of the rapids serenades you throughout the night. All 20 campsites require a short hike from a few hundred feet to over 0.5 mile to reach, but the riverside location is worth the effort. Since you must hike in to reach the campsites, the park asks that you check in at least 2 hours before dark, so you can get settled in your campsite before nightfall. Also, remember that this is black bear country, so be sure to practice proper food and trash storage, and bring plenty of rope along to string your food up. A wonderful grassy picnic area makes up the main body of the park, with several miles of hiking trails leading to the outreaches of the surrounding Mountain Bridge Wilderness. Even a waterfall aficionado like myself is thoroughly impressed with the features found along the rocky Jones Gap Trail. Five waterfalls over a 5-mile stretch of trail: quite remarkable. If you wish to explore even more territory, take a day trip over to Caesar's Head State Park. Caesar's Head is the sister park to Jones Gap and is home to nearly 35 miles of hiking trails. As for Jones Gap, the park is home to the remains of the Cleveland Fish Hatchery. This was the first fish hatchery in the state, and was in operation up until 1962. The trout pond still has several species of trout thriving in its chilly water. You can try your hand at fly fishing in the river and creeks nearby, provided you carry a South Carolina state fishing license. Bring a good book, dip your toes in the water, or simply peer through your binoculars for some outstanding bird watching. Although this peaceful park seems a bit remote, at the dead end of a deep country road, the tranquility found in this far-off location is quite calming. Please keep our state parks clean. I urge you to practice leave no trace camping. Pack it in, pack it out.

60 Table Rock State Park

Location: 158 E. Ellison Ln., Pickens; about 14 miles north of Pickens
Season: Year-round
Sites: 94; 3 group camping areas are also available and can accommodate from 36, 42, and 66 people each; backcountry camping and cabin rentals are also available
Maximum length: 45 feet, but there are a limited number of sites that can accommodate this size RV
Facilities: Flush toilets, hot showers, electric, water, fire rings, picnic tables, dump station, ice and firewood for sale, pet friendly
Fee per night: $$–$$$
Management: South Carolina Department of Natural Resources
Contact: (864) 878-9813; www.southcarolinaparks.com/tablerock/camping.aspx; for reservations call (866) 345-7275 or visit www.reserveamerica.com
Finding the campground: From the junction of SC 11 and SC 178 near Sunset, drive east on SC 11 for 4.1 miles to a left onto West Gate Road (SR 25) and travel for 0.4 mile to the entrance to the park on your right.

From the junction of SC 11 and SC 8 South, drive west on SC 11 for approximately 6.0 miles to a right onto West Gate Road (SR 25) and follow the directions above.

GPS coordinates: N35 01.408 / W82 42.309

Maps: *DeLorme: South Carolina Atlas and Gazetteer* page 17, E8

About the campground: For such a beautiful park, the campsites tend to be a bit close together, but the upper loop seems a little better than the lower. The park itself is huge and broken into several different sections. Most of the property surrounds two serene mountain lakes. A designated swim area is open seasonally during the summer months, and boat rentals can be found on Pinnacle Lake. Or you can use the boat ramp and launch your own nonmotorized boat on Lake Oolenoy. Two fishing piers are also on the latter lake, but you must obtain a South Carolina state fishing license before using your rod and reel. Several hiking trails can be found within the park, including one that takes you to Carrick Creek Falls, and one that leads to the top of Table Rock Mountain. If you prefer a longer hike, you can also access the famous Foothills Trail as it passes right through the park.

Lake Jocassee Area

Campground	Total sites	Hookup sites	Max. RV length	Hookups	Toilets	Showers	Drinking water	Dump station	Recreation	Fee	Reservations
61 **Keowee-Toxaway State Park**	25	10	40'	E, W	F	Y	Y	Y	H, S, F, B*, L*, P	$-$$	Y
62 **Devil's Fork State Park**	92	59	65'	E, W	F	Y	Y	Y	H, S, F, B, L, P, **	$$-$$$	Y

* See campground entry for specific information

61 Keowee-Toxaway State Park

Location: 108 Residence Dr., Sunset; about 17 miles northwest of Pickens
Season: Year-round
Sites: 10 RV sites; 14 tent sites; 1 backcountry group camp area is also available and can accommodate up to 25 people; individual backcountry camping is also available; 1 cabin rental is also available and can hold up to 10 people
Maximum length: 40 feet, but there are a limited number of sites that can accommodate this size RV
Facilities: Flush toilets, hot showers, electric, water, fire rings, picnic tables, dump station, pet friendly
Fee per night: $-$$
Management: South Carolina Department of Natural Resources
Contact: (864) 868-2605; www.southcarolinaparks.com/keoweetoxaway/camping.aspx; for reservations call (866) 345-7275 or visit www.reserveamerica.com
Finding the campground: From the junction of SC 11 and SC 133, drive west on SC 11 for 0.1 mile to a right onto Cabin Road (SR 347) at the entrance to the park.
From the junction of SC 11 and SC 130 near Salem, drive east on SC 11 for approximately 6.1 miles to a left onto Cabin Road (SR 347) at the entrance to the park.
GPS coordinates: N34 55.895 / W82 53.187
Maps: *DeLorme: South Carolina Atlas and Gazetteer* page 16, G5
About the campground: Split into two separate areas, the camping at Keowee-Toxaway State Park offers two different settings. Sitting high upon a spur, the RV campsites are surrounded by forest, yet surprisingly, despite their close proximity to Eastatoe Creek, none offer waterfront views. The tent sites have the typical amenities of a fire ring, picnic table, and tent pad, but the sites are literally right on top of each other, giving you virtually no privacy. The park itself is quite nice. A paved canoe and kayak launch gives you the opportunity to explore the many islands just a short paddle away. You can swim in the fresh mountain water, or fish from your boat or the banks, provided you acquire a South Carolina state fishing license. Several miles of hiking trails extend to the far reaches of the park, and the backcountry campsites can be reached via the hiking trails or by boat. The cabin rental is quite nice and worth a mention, but quite honestly if you plan on

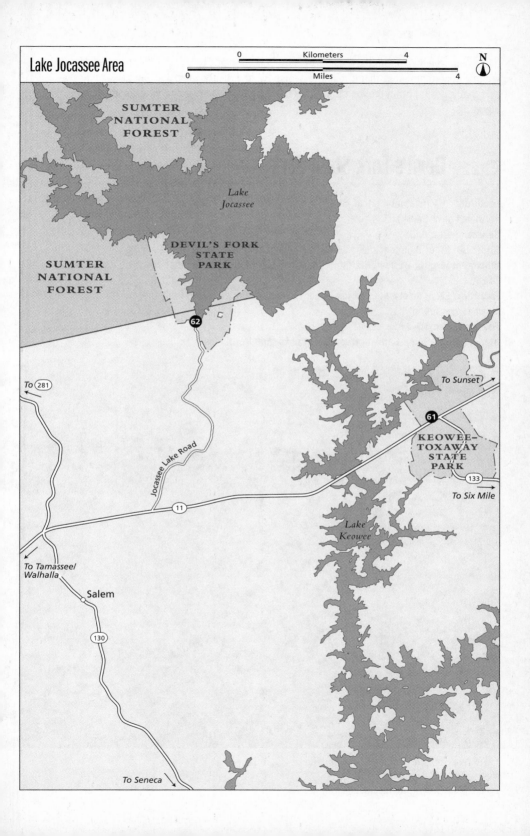

tent camping, either stay in the RV sites or head down the road to Devil's Fork State Park instead. Another important note is that if you have a large RV, or if the RV campsites are full, again I suggest that you head down the road to Devil's Fork State Park, where they can accommodate the bigger rigs.

62 Devil's Fork State Park

Location: 161 Holcombe Circle, Salem; about 7 miles northwest of Pickens, and about 15 miles northeast of Walhalla
Season: Year-round
Sites: 59; 20 walk-in tent sites; 13 boat-in sites; cabin rentals are also available
Maximum length: 65 feet, but there are a limited number of sites that can accommodate this size RV
Facilities: Flush toilets, hot showers, electric, water, fire rings, picnic tables, dump station, laundry facilities, pet friendly
Fee per night: $$-$$$
Management: South Carolina Department of Natural Resources

Lake Jocassee is a perfect place to paddle.

Contact: (864) 944-2639; www.southcarolina parks.com/devilsfork/camping.aspx; for reservations call (866) 345-7275 or visit www.reserveamerica.com

Finding the campground: From the junction of SC 11 and SC 130 near Salem, drive east on SC 11 for 1.6 miles to a left onto Jocassee Lake Road at the sign for Devil's Fork State Park. Travel for 3.5 miles to the park at the end of the road.

From the junction of SC 11 and SC 133 near Keowee-Toxaway State Park, drive west on SC 11 for approximately 4.6 miles to a right onto Jocassee Lake Road and follow the directions above.

GPS coordinates: N34 57.075 / W82 56.904

Maps: *DeLorme: South Carolina Atlas and Gazetteer* page 16, F4

About the campground: Hilly, wooded campsites overlook Lake Jocassee through the trees. This magnificent park has so much to offer, and therefore stays busy throughout the week. As expected, the lakefront campsites tend to

A raccoon peeks out from behind the trash dumpster.

be a bit crowded. But silence and solitude are not the main reason you came to visit Devil's Fork State Park. It's to enjoy the amazingly clear green water of Lake Jocassee. Spreading out over 7,500 acres, the lake is fed by four mountain rivers flowing down from North Carolina. The park has four boat ramps, giving you ample opportunity to explore the outer reaches of this wonderful body of water. Laurel Fork Falls sits at the far northeastern end of the lake and can be reached by boat only. Or you can experience boat-in camping at one of the park's thirteen campsites that rest across the lake at the foot of Musterground Mountain. Trophy fish flourish in the lake, and fishing is allowed, provided you attain a South Carolina state fishing license. Swimming is also permitted at your own risk. Surprisingly, Lake Jocassee is a popular SCUBA diving destination, with typical visibility of 15 to 50 feet. There's a delightful concession stand overlooking the lake. This privately run pavilion sells food, drinks, and sundry items such as books and sunscreen. They also have limited camping gear, and rent out canopies and chairs for a perfect day of lying out on the grassy hill beside the water. But that's not all. They also rent canoes and kayaks, pontoon boats, and even carry stand-up paddleboards (SUPs) boards for rent, giving visitors plenty of ways to get out and appreciate the lake firsthand. For advance reservations on rentals, contact the Eclectic Sun concession directly at (864) 944-1191 or visit their website at www.eclecticsun.com. If you simply want to enjoy the waterfront view, but prefer to stay on dry land, the park has picnic shelters and playgrounds. If hiking is your thing, the park has a few trails within the park boundary, or you can head out deep into the forest into the neighboring Ellicott Rock Wilderness Area. Several waterfalls are within easy reach, the closest of which are just up the road in North Carolina, off NC 281. *FalconGuides: Hiking Waterfalls in North Carolina* is a great book to help you find them. With so much to do, and the astonishing beauty of a mountain lake at your doorstep, Devil's Fork State Park easily makes the Author's Favorites list.

Seneca Area

Campground	Total sites	Hookup sites	Max. RV length	Hookups	Toilets	Showers	Drinking water	Dump station	Recreation	Fee	Reservations
63 **Mile Creek County Park**	69	69	40'	E, W	F	Y	Y	Y	S, F, B, L, BB, V, P	$$-$$$	Y
64 **High Falls County Park**	100	100	35'	E, W	F	Y	Y	Y	S, F, B, L, T, BB, HS, MG, V, P, **	$$-$$$	N
65 **South Cove County Park**	86	86	40'	E, W	F	Y	Y	Y	S, F, B, L, T, BB, V, HS, P	$$-$$$	N

* See campground entry for specific information

63 Mile Creek County Park

Location: 757 Keowee Baptist Church Rd., Six Mile
Season: Year-round
Sites: 69
Maximum length: 40 feet
Facilities: Flush toilets, hot showers, electric, water, fire rings, picnic tables, dump station, ice and firewood for sale, pet friendly
Fee per night: $$-$$$
Management: Pickens County Parks and Recreation
Contact: (864) 868-2196; www.co.pickens.sc.us/MileCreekPark/default.aspx
Finding the campground: From the junction of SC 133 and SC 11 near Sunset, drive south on SC 133 for 7.7 miles to a right onto Keowee Baptist Church Road (SR 327) at the sign for Mile Creek Park and travel for 2.0 miles to where the road ends at the entrance to the park.

From the junction of SC 133 and SC 183 near Six Mile, drive north on SC 133 for 1.9 miles to a left onto Keowee Baptist Church Road (SR 327) at the sign for Mile Creek Park and follow the directions above.
GPS coordinates: N34 51.426 / W82 52.912
Maps: *DeLorme: South Carolina Atlas and Gazetteer* page 16, H5
About the campground: Lake Keowee renders you speechless at this delightful county park. The vivid green water in contrast with the red clay of the shoreline is jaw dropping. The fact that this park is less frequented than the other two Pickens County–run campgrounds makes this even more enjoyable. Mile Creek Park has all the usual amenities of a local community park, with waterfront playgrounds and picnic shelters, a swim beach, and a boat ramp. If you prefer to stay on dry land, they have a basketball net and volleyball net too. Or you can take a quick jaunt over to Pickens and visit the Hagood Grist Mill or the Pickens County Museum. The campground at Mile Creek sits on a small, hilly peninsula, with every site within clear view of the lake. Most sit just a stone's throw from the water's edge. They are a bit close together, but once again, the

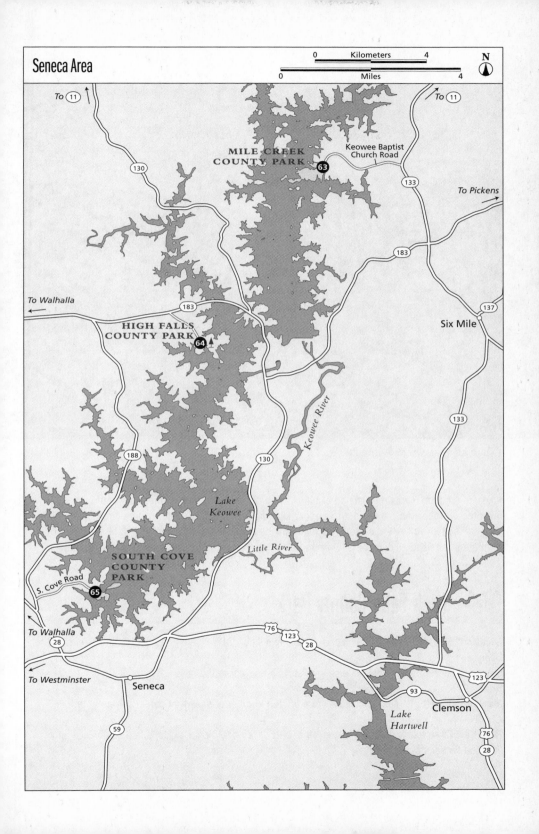

0 Kilometers 4

0 Miles 4

N

To 11

To 11

MILE CREEK
COUNTY PARK

63

Keowee Baptist
Church Road

130

133

To Pickens

183

To Walhalla

183

HIGH FALLS
COUNTY PARK

64

137

Six Mile

Keowee River

188

133

130

Lake
Keowee

Little River

SOUTH COVE
COUNTY PARK

S. Cove Road

65

To Walhalla

76

123

28

28

To Westminster

Seneca

123

93

59

Lake
Hartwell

Clemson

76

28

Camp along the peaceful shores of Lake Keowee.

lakeside location eases the tension of being overcrowded, and I still count this one among my favorites. Whether you paddle out to explore island after island, or cast a fishing line right from your campsite, you are bound to enjoy the many pleasures of Mile Creek Park. Note, a South Carolina state fishing license is required whether you fish from the shores or from your boat.

64 High Falls County Park

Location: 671 High Falls Rd., Seneca; about 8 miles east of Walhalla and about 10 miles north of Seneca
Season: Mar 1–mid-Nov (the day-use area stays open year-round)
Sites: 100
Maximum length: 35 feet, but there are a limited number of sites that can accommodate this size RV
Facilities: Flush toilets, hot showers, electric, water, fire rings, picnic tables, dump station, ice and firewood for sale, pet friendly

Fee per night: $$–$$$
Management: Oconee County Parks and Recreation
Contact: (864) 888-1488 or (864) 882-8234; www.oconeecountry.com/highsouthparks.html
Finding the campground: From the junction of SC 183 and SC 188 near Walhalla, drive east on SC 183 for 1.6 miles to a right onto High Falls Road at the sign for High Falls County Park and travel for 1.0 mile to the park at the end of the road.

From the junction of SC 183 and SC 130 West near Old Pickens, drive west on SC 183 for 1.9 miles to a left onto High Falls Road at the sign for High Falls County Park and follow the directions above.

GPS coordinates: N34 47.820 / W82 55.763
Maps: *DeLorme: South Carolina Atlas and Gazetteer* page 22, A5
About the campground:

Fabulous! Just fabulous. Each time I visit High Falls Park, I'm more impressed than the last. A multitude of activities coupled with the natural beauty of Lake Keowee is simply awe-inspiring. Swim, fish, or launch your boat into the crisp, green water, and then pull it right up to one of the ten waterfront campsites. They have tennis, volleyball, basketball, baseball, horseshoe pits, a sandy beach area that is a designated swim area, and even a putt-putt mini golf course. The campsites are clean but crowded. But given the lakeshore location, the crowding can be overlooked. The park store is a lovely historic building built in the 1830s and has sundry items for sale that you may have left behind. One last note of importance: Don't be fooled by the park's name. There is no waterfall on the property. High Falls did exist many years ago, when the water levels were lower, but since then the lake has risen, covering over and drowning out what was once known as High Falls.

A gorgeous horse grazes on the grass.

65 South Cove County Park

Location: 1099 South Cove Rd., Seneca; along the shores of Lake Keowee, about 2 miles north of Seneca and about 7 miles southeast of Walhalla
Season: Year-round
Sites: 86
Maximum length: 40 feet, but there are a limited number of sites that can accommodate this size RV
Facilities: Flush toilets, hot showers, electric, water, fire rings, picnic tables, dump station, ice and firewood for sale, pet friendly
Fee per night: $$-$$$
Management: Oconee County Parks and Recreation
Contact: (864) 882-5250; www.oconeecountry.com/highsouthparks.html
Finding the campground: From the junction of SC 188 and SC 28 in Seneca, drive north on SC 188 for 0.2 mile to a right onto South Cove Road and travel for 1.5 miles to the park at the end of the road.

From the junction of SC 188 and SC 183 near Walhalla, drive south on SC 188 for 4.9 miles to a stop sign. Continue straight through the intersection, following SC 188 for another 3.1 miles to a left onto South Cove Road at the sign for South Cove County Park and follow the directions above.
GPS coordinates: N34 42.852 / W82 58.045
Maps: *DeLorme: South Carolina Atlas and Gazetteer* page 22, B4
About the campground: The day-use area in this popular local park is heavily used by the community. With tennis, basketball, volleyball, horseshoe pits, and boat ramps it's no wonder. You can swim at your own risk, but there is no designated swim area per se. Or launch your boat and explore the far reaches of the lake. You can fish from your boat or the banks as long as you have a South Carolina state fishing license. Along with the many activities, the good news is that the campground itself is isolated from the day-use area. But don't get your hopes up too high, for it too stays busy on any night of the week. Nearly half the campsites sit right upon the banks of Lake Keowee, but they are very close together, with little or no tree cover to separate you from your neighbor. As you settle in by the fire, if you accept and appreciate the beauty of the lake with its crisp green water, it helps you overlook the lack of privacy that you have in this wide-open setting.

Camp right on the water's edge at South Cove County Park.

Clemson Area

Campground	Total sites	Hookup sites	Max. RV length	Hookups	Toilets	Showers	Drinking water	Dump station	Recreation	Fee	Reservations
66 **Twin Lakes Campground**	102	102	62'	E, W	F	Y	Y	Y	S, F, B, L, P	$$$	Y
67 **Clemson University's Eagle's Nest Tree House**	1	0	n/a	N	V	N	Y	N	H, BB, HS, DG, V, P	$$$	Y*
68 **Oconee Point Campground**	71	71	60'	E, W	F	Y	Y	Y	S, F, B, L, P	$$$	Y
69 **Coneross Campground**	107	95	76'	E, W	F	Y	Y	Y	S, F, B, L, P	$$-$$$	Y

* See campground entry for specific information

66   Twin Lakes Campground

Location: 140 Winnebago Trail, Pendleton; about 5 miles south of Clemson, and about 14 miles northwest of Anderson

Season: 1 loop is open year-round; the entire campground is open Apr 1–Nov 30

Sites: 102

Maximum length: 62 feet, but there are a limited number of sites that can accommodate this size RV

Facilities: Flush toilets, hot showers, electric, water, fire rings, charcoal grills, picnic tables, lantern holders, dump station, pet friendly

Fee per night: $$$

Management: US Army Corps of Engineers

Contact: (888) 893-0678; www.sas.usace.army.mil/About/DivisionsandOffices/Operations Division/HartwellDamandLake/PlanAVisit/Camping.aspx; for reservations, call (877) 444-6777 or visit www.recreation.gov

Finding the campground: From I-85 get off at exit 14 and drive north on SC 187 for approximately 2.8 miles to a left onto Fants Grove Road (SR 1098) at the sign for Twin Lakes Recreation Area. Travel for 3.8 miles to a left onto Twin Lakes Road and drive 1.0 mile to the entrance to the campground on your right.

From the junction of US 76 and SC 93 in Clemson, drive east on US 76 for approximately 2.6 miles to a right onto West Queen Street. Follow West Queen Street (which becomes Twin Lakes Road) for 2.4 miles to the entrance to the campground on the right.

GPS coordinates: N34 37.676 / W82 50.967

Maps: *DeLorme: South Carolina Atlas and Gazetteer* page 23, D6

About the campground: As you drive down Twin Lakes Road, the mountains come into view off in the distance. That, combined with its close proximity to Clemson University, keeps this popular destination busy throughout the year. I highly recommend that you make reservations ahead of

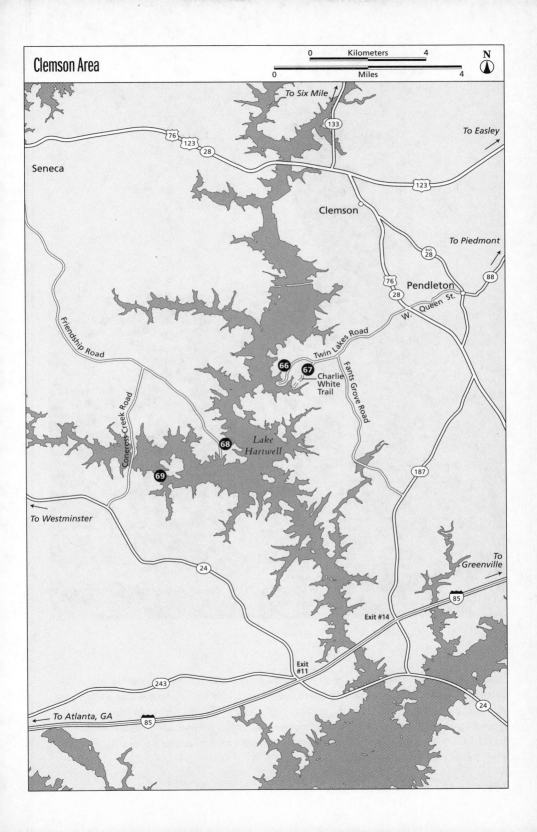

Clemson Area

Seneca

Clemson

Pendleton

To Six Mile

To Easley

To Piedmont

To Greenville

To Westminster

To Atlanta, GA

Kilometers

Miles

N

76
123
28
133
123
28
88
76
28

W. Queen St.

Friendship Road

Twin Lakes Road

Charlie White Trail

Fants Grove Road

Concross Creek Road

Lake Hartwell

66
67
68
69

187

24

85

85

243

24

Exit #14

Exit #11

An anhinga soaks up the sun.

time, especially on the weekends. The sites are a bit more crowded than the other campgrounds on Lake Hartwell, but as is typical to the area, almost every single campsite is on the water's edge. You can boat right up to your site, and the park's very busy boat ramp is isolated from the campground, so you don't have to deal with that heavy traffic as you sip your coffee in your lakefront haven. There's a courtesy dock for visitors with boats and a swim beach for those who prefer to enjoy the calming water from the shore.

67 Clemson University's Eagle's Nest Tree House

Location: About 5 miles south of Clemson, and about 14 miles northwest of Anderson
Season: Mid-August–late May
Sites: 1 rustic "cabin" can accommodate up to 12 people; 16 other cabins less rustic are also available
Maximum length: n/a
Facilities: Vault toilet, water spigot, fire ring, no pets allowed
Fee per night: $$$
Management: Clemson University
Contact: (864) 646-7502
Finding the tree house: From I-85 get off at exit 14 and drive north on SC 187 for approximately 2.8 miles to a left onto Fants Grove Road (SR 1098) at the sign for Twin Lakes Recreation Area. Travel for 3.8 miles to a left onto Twin Lakes Road and drive 0.5 mile to a left onto Charlie White Trail, at the entrance to the Outdoor Lab.

From the junction of US 76 and SC 93 in Clemson, drive east on US 76 for approximately 2.6 miles to a right onto West Queen Street. Follow West Queen Street (which becomes Twin Lakes Road) for 1.9 miles to a left onto Charlie White Trail, at the entrance to the Outdoor Lab.
GPS coordinates: N34 37.548 / W82 50.560
Maps: *DeLorme: South Carolina Atlas and Gazetteer* page 23, D6
About the tree house: We all know the familiar orange paw of the Clemson Tigers. But few are aware that Clemson has a property, remote from the college, known as the "Outdoor Lab."

The Lab sits along the banks of Lake Hartwell and offers students and guests a relaxing, forested place to get away from the hustle and bustle of it all. The accommodations are primarily cabins, but they also have one dwelling known as the "Eagle's Nest." A short, wide trail heads northeast from the main road and leads campers to this large structure touted as Clemson's tree house. Although it's not actually what I would consider a real tree house, it does sit nestled away among the trees and is quite a unique form of lodging. The bottom half is a large, covered seating area with benches all around it, and the upstairs is a half-screened sleeping quarters with mats covering the floor to cushion the surface. The "tree house" sleeps up to 12 people and is open to the public. There's a water spigot, fire ring, and an outhouse dedicated just for those staying here. Although some may not consider this "real" camping, it's a very cool alternative, in which you still get to sleep outdoors, but have protection from the elements. There are activities galore on the property, so you won't be at a loss for things to do. Along with hiking, they have basketball, volleyball, horseshoe pits, picnic areas, and a disc golf course. Reservations are required. Check with the park when you make your reservation, because certain activities may not be available to the public when other groups are on-site.

68 Oconee Point Campground

Location: 200 Oconee Point Rd., Seneca; about 15 miles northwest of Anderson, and about 7 miles southeast of Seneca
Season: May 1–Sept 30
Sites: 71
Maximum length: 60 feet, but there are a limited number of sites that can accommodate this size RV
Facilities: Flush toilets, hot showers, electric, water, fire rings, charcoal grills, picnic tables, lantern holders, dump station, pet friendly
Fee per night: $$$
Management: US Army Corps of Engineers
Contact: (888) 893-0678; www.sas.usace.army.mil/About/DivisionsandOffices/Operations Division/HartwellDamandLake/PlanAVisit/Camping.aspx; for reservations, call (877) 444-6777 or visit www.recreation.gov.

A reminder of simpler times.

Finding the campground: From I-85, get off at exit 11 and drive north on SC 24 for approximately 6.2 miles to a right onto Coneross Creek Road. Travel for 3.3 miles to a right onto Friendship Road (SR 21). Follow Friendship Road for 2.3 miles to a left onto Oconee Point Road. Travel for 0.15 mile to the entrance to the campground at the end of the road.

From the junction of SC 24 and SC 59 in Tokeena, drive south on SC 24 for approximately 4.2 miles to a left onto Coneross Creek Road and follow the directions above.

GPS coordinates: N34 36.111 / W82 52.281

Maps: *DeLorme: South Carolina Atlas and Gazetteer* page 22, D5

About the campground: Once again the Army Corps of Engineers (ACE) has found the perfect location for its facility. The Oconee Point Campground sits out on a peninsula near the mouth of the Seneca River, on a northwestern arm of Lake Hartwell. As a result of this ideal locale, almost every campsite is waterfront. But unfortunately, they tend to lack privacy. Stunning sunrises and sunsets greet you as you step out of your tent or RV, take just a few steps, and dip your toes in the pristine water. As with most of the ACE campgrounds, the lake is the highlight, and the amenities include a boat ramp, courtesy dock, and swim beach. Fishing is allowed from the banks or boat, but before you launch your lure, make sure you have your South Carolina state fishing license. Clemson University is within easy reach on the east side of the lake, and access to I-85 is close enough to be convenient but far enough away to not hear the sound of the traffic as it's carried across the water.

69 Coneross Campground

Location: 699 Coneross Park Rd., Townville; about 15 miles northwest of Anderson, and about 7 miles southeast of Seneca

Season: May 1–Sept 30

Sites: 107

Maximum length: 76 feet, but there are a limited number of sites that can accommodate this size RV

Facilities: Flush toilets, hot showers, electric, water, fire rings, charcoal grills, picnic tables, lantern holders, dump station, pet friendly

Fee per night: $$–$$$

Management: US Army Corps of Engineers

Contact: (888) 893-0678; www.sas.usace.army.mil/About/DivisionsandOffices/Operations Division/HartwellDamandLake/PlanAVisit/Camping.aspx; for reservations, call (877) 444-6777 or visit www.recreation.gov

Finding the campground: From I-85, get off at exit 11 and drive north on SC 24 for approximately 6.2 miles to a right onto Coneross Creek Road. Travel for 0.6 mile to a right onto Perry Woolbright Road, and then immediately turn left onto Coneross Park Road. Travel for 0.7 mile to the entrance to the campground at the end of the road.

From the junction of SC 24 and SC 59 North in Tokeena, drive south on SC 24 for approximately 4.2 miles to a left onto Coneross Creek Road, and follow the directions above.

GPS coordinates: N34 35.464 / W82 53.793

Maps: *DeLorme: South Carolina Atlas and Gazetteer* page 22, D5

Bales of hay are a common sight in the country.

About the campground: Wooded sites greet you at this lakefront campground. Although several of the campsites are on the water, there are not as many as most other Army Corps of Engineers campgrounds on Lake Hartwell. You do, however, have tree cover, which gives you privacy from your neighbors and shade from the heat of the day. The trees also harbor many bird species that can be heard singing throughout the day. A boat ramp and courtesy dock are on the property but not near the campground, so you don't have to hear the boat ramp traffic coming and going. There are two swim beaches, and you can fish from the banks or your boat, provided you have a South Carolina state fishing license.

Anderson Area

Campground	Total sites	Hookup sites	Max. RV length	Hookups	Toilets	Showers	Drinking water	Dump station	Recreation	Fee	Reservations
70 **Springfield Campground**	79	79	50'	E, W	F	Y	Y	Y	S, F, B, L, G*, P	$$$	Y
71 **Sadlers Creek State Park**	71	52	66'	E, W	F	Y	Y	Y	H, M, S, F, B, L, V, BB, P	$$	Y
72 **Crescent Group Camp**	32	32	40'	E, W	F	Y	Y	Y	S, F, B, L*, P	$$$	Y
73 **Lake Hartwell State Park**	128	116	45'	E, W	F	Y	Y	Y	H, S, F, B, L, BB, P	$$-$$$	Y

* See campground entry for specific information

70 Springfield Campground

Location: 1915 Providence Church Rd., Anderson; about 9 miles southwest of Anderson, and about 5 miles north of the South Carolina/Georgia state line
Season: Apr 1–Oct 31
Sites: 79
Maximum length: 50 feet, but there are a limited number of sites that can accommodate this size RV
Facilities: Flush toilets, hot showers, electric, water, fire rings, picnic tables, lantern holders, dump station, pet friendly
Fee per night: $$$
Management: US Army Corps of Engineers
Contact: (888) 893-0678; www.sas.usace.army.mil/About/DivisionsandOffices/Operations Division/HartwellDamandLake/PlanAVisit/Camping.aspx; for reservations, call (877) 444-6777 or visit www.recreation.gov
Finding the campground: From I-85 get off at exit 14 and travel south on SC 187 for 1.3 miles to a stoplight at SC 24. Go left here, continuing to follow SC 187/24 east for approximately 3.0 miles to a right onto SC 187 South. Follow SC 187 south for 4.2 miles to a right onto Providence Church Road and travel for 2.1 miles to a left onto Springfield Road. Travel for 0.15 mile to the entrance to the campground at the end of the road.

From the junction of SC 187 and US 29 near the South Carolina/Georgia state line, drive north on SC 187 for 3.7 miles to a left onto Providence Church Road at the sign for Springfield Campground, and follow the directions above.
GPS coordinates: N34 26.784 / W82 49.324
Maps: *DeLorme: South Carolina Atlas and Gazetteer* page 23, G6

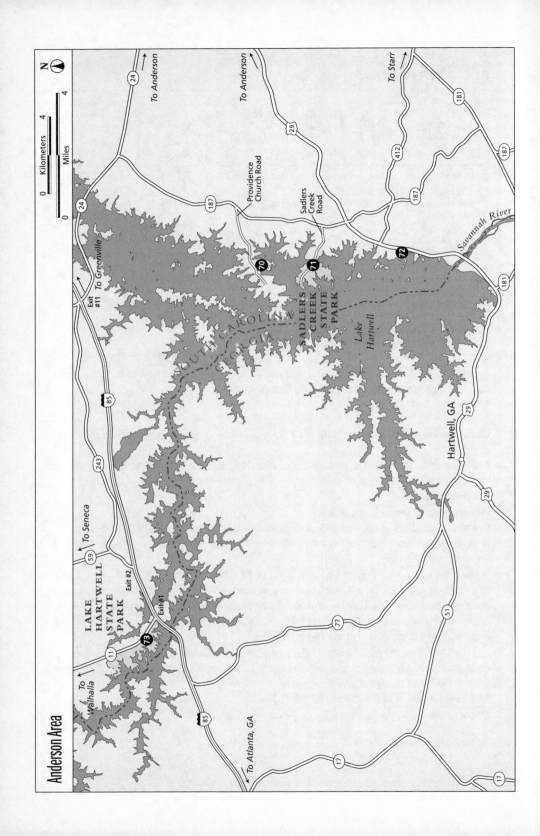

Anderson Area

What a great place to sit on a swing.

About the campground: The campsites at Springfield are delightful. With patches of trees in between, they give you plenty of privacy from other campers. Almost every site is on the water, resting along the banks of Lake Hartwell. You are given beautiful opportunities to watch the sunrise and sunset daily. Fish, boat, swim at the beach, or just sit on a swing and enjoy the serene setting that Springfield has to offer. With a boat ramp and a courtesy dock on the property, there's easy access to launch your watercraft and explore this man-made reservoir at length. If you prefer to stay on dry land, there's a golf course just up the road, so be sure to bring your clubs along.

71 Sadlers Creek State Park

Location: 940 Sadlers Creek Rd., Anderson; about 12 miles southwest of Anderson
Season: Year-round
Sites: 52 RV sites; 14 rustic tent sites; 5 group camp areas are also available and can accommodate up to 50 people each
Maximum length: 66 feet, but there are a limited number of sites that can accommodate this size RV
Facilities: Flush toilets, hot showers, electric, water, fire rings, picnic tables, dump station, pet friendly
Fee per night: $$
Management: South Carolina Department of Natural Resources
Contact: (864) 226-8950; www.southcarolinaparks.com/sadlerscreek/camping.aspx; for reservations call (866) 345-7275 or visit www.reserveamerica.com
Finding the campground: From I-85 get off at exit 14 and travel south on SC 187 for 1.3 miles to a stoplight at SC 24. Go left here, continuing to follow SC 187/24 east for approximately 3.0

The sunsets are exquisite on Lake Hartwell.

Mikey settles in for the evening at Sadlers Creek State Park.

miles to a right onto SC 187 South. Follow SC 187 south for 7.2 miles to a right onto Sadlers Creek Road (SR 741). Travel for 1.2 miles to the entrance to the park.

From the junction of SC 187 and US 29 near Holland Store, drive north on SC 187 for 0.8 mile to the entrance to the park on the left.

GPS coordinates: N34 25.343 / W82 49.279

Maps: *DeLorme: South Carolina Atlas and Gazetteer* page 23, G6

About the campground: Bring the family and leave the stress of the city behind. Sadlers Creek has activities galore for all to enjoy by boat or by shore. With volleyball, basketball, playgrounds and picnics, hiking and mountain bike trails, and even a baseball field, there's something for everyone. Not to mention the obvious, swimming, fishing, boating, and a boat ramp. Stunning sunrises and sunsets greet you daily. That, combined with lakefront campsites, makes this picture-perfect place an Author's Favorite. You do hear the occasional gunshot in the distance or the hum of a boat motor in the early morning hours as the anglers head out for the day. But that's a small price to pay for paradise. Deer abound throughout the recreational area, especially at dusk and dawn, so be sure to take your time, drive slowly, and take in the scenery.

72 Crescent Group Camp

Location: Campers Way, Starr; off US 29; about 14 miles southwest of Anderson, and about 8 miles east of Hartwell, Georgia
Season: May 1–Sept 30
Sites: 2 group campsite loops: Loop A has 10 sites and can accommodate up to 100 people; Loop B has 22 sites and can accommodate up to 220 people
Maximum length: Loop A, 40 feet; Loop B, 35 feet
Facilities: Flush toilets, hot showers, electric, water, fire rings, charcoal grills, picnic tables, lantern holders, trash cans, dump station, pet friendly
Fee per night: $$$
Management: US Army Corps of Engineers
Contact: (888) 893-0678; www.sas.usace.army.mil/About/DivisionsandOffices/Operations Division/HartwellDamandLake/PlanAVisit/Camping.aspx; for reservations, call (877) 444-6777 or visit www.recreation.gov
Finding the campground: From the junction of US 29 and SC 187, drive south on US 29 for 2.0 miles to a hard right onto SR 180 at the sign for Crescent Group Campground. Travel for less than 0.1 mile and turn left onto Campers Way. Follow this for 0.1 mile to the entrance to the campground.

From the junction of US 29 and the South Carolina/Georgia state line, drive north on US 29 for approximately 1.9 miles to the entrance to the campground on your right.
GPS coordinates: N34 22.880 / W82 48.809
Maps: *DeLorme: South Carolina Atlas and Gazetteer* page 23, H6
About the campground: Wow, group camping at its best! Unlike the typical group camp, which has a large open area for groups to pitch multiple tents upon, Crescent Campground offers group camping, but it's broken down into individual campsites just like a conventional campground. Not only do campers get their own individual campsite, but every site on the property is waterfront, resting right on the shores of Lake Hartwell. This unique layout lets you appreciate the company of your friends, yet still have lots of privacy to enjoy the amazing views of both the sunrise and sunset. If this isn't enough incentive, each site also has its own water and electric hookup. Groups can rent one loop or both, and each loop has a centrally located group shelter. Whether you swim, fish, or anchor your boat right beside your campsite, this place gives you the perfect opportunity to appreciate Lake Hartwell at its best. Although there's no boat ramp on the property, you can head over to the Singing Pines day use area, or to the nearby Big Water Marina to launch your boat. Big Water is a full-service marina that's open to the public, and if you don't have a boat of your own, they have rentals available. With a matchless layout and location, Crescent Group Camp is by far my favorite group camp in the state.

Crescent Group Camp offers some of the best group camping in the state.

73 Lake Hartwell State Park

Location: 19138-A Hwy. 11 S, Fair Play; about 12 miles south of Westminster, and about 20 miles west of Anderson
Season: 1 loop is open year-round; the rest of the campsites are open Apr 1–Nov 1
Sites: 128; cabin rentals are also available
Maximum length: 45 feet
Facilities: Flush toilets, hot showers, electric, water, fire rings, picnic tables, dump station, ice and firewood for sale, pet friendly
Fee per night: $$–$$$
Management: South Carolina Department of Natural Resources
Contact: (864) 972-3352; www.southcarolinaparks.com/lakehartwell/camping.aspx; for reservations call (866) 345-7275 or visit www.reserveamerica.com
Finding the campground: From I-85 get off at South Carolina exit 1 and drive north on SC 11 for 0.5 mile to the entrance to the park on the left.

From the junction of SC 11 and SC 24 near Westminster, drive south on SC 11 for 9.3 miles to the entrance to the park on your right.
GPS coordinates: N34 29.673 / W83 01.905
Maps: *DeLorme: South Carolina Atlas and Gazetteer* page 22, F4
About the campground: Rolling hills give this park a unique feel compared to the other campgrounds that rest upon the shores of Lake Hartwell, but these hills also limit campers from direct lakefront access. While you can see the lake from most of the campsites, many overlook the water from high above. The park is wooded, so there's a moderate amount of privacy from site to site, depending on which loop you're in. A short walk leads you into the tent sites, which are the only sites in the campground that sit right on the pristine water's edge. One loop is open year-round, while the other loops open from Apr 1 to Nov 1. There's a basketball net and a short nature trail, but clearly the highlight of the park is the lake itself. The camp store has loaner life vests and fishing rods, but you must obtain a South Carolina state fishing license before you cast your line. Two boat ramps grace the property, and although there is no actual designated swim area, swimming is allowed at your own risk. There are a few perks not seen at most other campgrounds in the state, including a laundry room that's open to campers and a wi-fi connection in the visitor's center. All in all, this is a great park with an even greater location.

Westminster Area

Campground	Total sites	Hookup sites	Max. RV length	Hookups	Toilets	Showers	Drinking water	Dump station	Recreation	Fee	Reservations
74 Chau Ram County Park	26	26	35'	E, W	F	Y	Y	Y	H, M, F, Tu, P	$$$	N
75 Brasstown Falls Primitive Campsites	2	0	n/a	N	N	N	N	N	H, F	No Fee	N
76 Woodall Shoals Primitive Campsites	4	0	n/a	N	V	N	N	N	H, R, F, P	No Fee	N
77 Thrifts Ferry Primitive Campsite	2	0	n/a	N	N	N	N	N	H, B*, L*	No Fee	N
78 Double Branch Primitive Campsite	1	0	n/a	N	N	N	N	N	H, F	No Fee	N
79 Cassidy Bridge Hunt Camp	1	0	n/a	N	V	N	N	N	H, R, F, B*	$-$$$	Y
80 Fall Creek Primitive Campsite	1	0	n/a	N	N	N	N	N	H, F	No Fee	N
81 Turpin Branch Primitive Campsite	1	0	n/a	N	N	N	N	N	H, F	No Fee	N
82 Grapevine Primitive Campground	15	0	n/a	N	V	N	N	N	H, F	No Fee	N
83 Blackwell Bridge Primitive Campsite	1	0	n/a	N	N	N	N	N	H, F	No Fee	N
84 Whetstone Horse Camp	18	0	None	N	V	N	Y	N	H, R, F, B*, L*	$$	Y
85 Timmy Place Primitive Campsite	1	0	n/a	N	N	N	N	N	H, R, F, B*, L*	No Fee	N

* See campground entry for specific information

74 Chau Ram County Park

Location: 1220 Chau Ram Park Rd., Westminster
Season: Mar 1–mid-Nov (contact the park for specific dates); be advised, the entire park closes during the winter months, even the day-use area
Sites: 26
Maximum length: 35 feet, but there are a limited number of sites that can accommodate this size RV
Facilities: Flush toilets, hot showers, electric, water, fire rings, charcoal grills, picnic tables, dump station, firewood for sale, pet friendly
Fee per night: $$$
Management: Oconee County Parks and Recreation

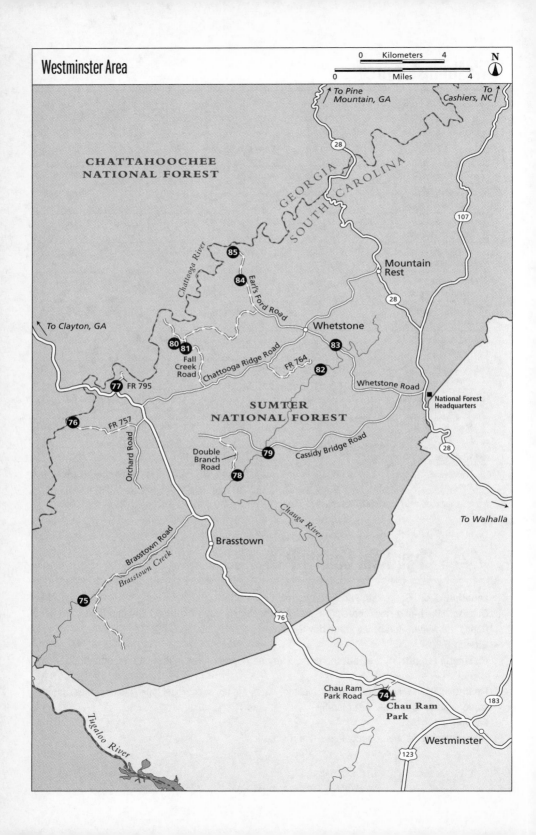

Westminster Area

0 Kilometers 4
0 Miles 4

N

To Pine Mountain, GA
To Cashiers, NC

CHATTAHOOCHEE NATIONAL FOREST

GEORGIA

SOUTH CAROLINA

28

107

Mountain Rest

28

Chattooga River

85

84

Earl's Ford Road

Whetstone

83

80 81

Fall Creek Road

Chattooga Ridge Road

FR 764

82

To Clayton, GA

77 FR 795

Whetstone Road

National Forest Headquarters

76

FR 757

Orchard Road

SUMTER NATIONAL FOREST

Double Branch Road

79

Cassidy Bridge Road

78

28

To Walhalla

Chauga River

Brasstown Road

Brasstown

Brasstown Creek

75

76

Tugaloo River

Chau Ram Park Road

74

Chau Ram Park

183

Westminster

123

Ramsey Falls is just a short walk from the campground at Chau Ram County Park.

Contact: (864) 647-9286; www.scmountainlakes.com/uploads/Lodging/CampSites.asp

Finding the campground: From the junction of US 76 and US 441 (in Clayton, Georgia), drive east on US 76 for 22.8 miles to a right turn onto Chau Ram Park Road. After turning onto the park road, follow it for 0.3 mile to the main entrance to the park.

From the junction of US 76 and the Chattooga River Bridge (Georgia/South Carolina state line), drive east on US 76 for 14.8 miles to a right turn onto Chau Ram Park Road and follow the directions above.

From the junction of US 76 and US 123 in Westminster, drive west on US 76 for 2.4 miles to a left turn onto Chau Ram Park Road and follow the directions above.

GPS coordinates: N34 40.929 / W83 08.710

Maps: *DeLorme: South Carolina Atlas and Gazetteer* page 22, C3

About the campground: The highlight of this small local park is easily Ramsey Falls and the Chauga River. Visitors can drive right up to the base of this delightful 30-foot waterfall, and watch the creek flawlessly flow by on its way to the river. Picnic to the sound of the water rushing by, or watch the kids as they play in the playground. You can rest your feet as you sit in the quaint gazebo, or take a hike or bike alongside the banks of the river. Tubing is popular in the area, and several whitewater rafting outfitters are nearby. After passing through the day-use area of this petite park, you arrive at the campground. Built up on a hillside, the sites are paved and have the typical amenities. But, unfortunately, they are quite crowded, and placed one right next to the other. So don't expect too much privacy as you sit by the fire. Also, due to the layout of the campground, it may take a bit of maneuvering to get the larger size RVs in your site. If you're not comfortable with this, or if you have an RV greater than 35 feet, head over to Oconee Point, Coneross, South Cove, or High Falls Campgrounds, or down to Lake Hartwell, or up to Oconee State Park.

75 Brasstown Falls Primitive Campsites

Location: About 13 miles west/northwest of Westminster, and about 8 miles west/south of the South Carolina/Georgia state line
Season: Year-round
Sites: 2
Maximum length: n/a
Facilities: Primitive fire rings, pet friendly
Fee per night: None
Management: Sumter National Forest–Andrew Pickens District
Contact: (864) 638-9568; www.fs.usda.gov/recarea/scnfs/recreation/camping-cabins/recarea/?recid=77596&actid=29
Finding the campsites: From the junction of US 76 and the Chattooga River Bridge (Georgia/South Carolina state line), drive east on US 76 for 5.6 miles to a right turn onto Brasstown Road. After turning onto Brasstown Road, travel for 3.9 miles to a right turn onto FR 751, just before crossing the small bridge over Brasstown Creek. After turning onto FR 751, travel for 0.4 mile to where the road dead-ends at the trailhead.
From the junction of US 76 and US 123 in Westminster, drive west on US 76 for 11.6 miles to a left turn onto Brasstown Road. After turning onto Brasstown Road, follow above directions.
Note: At 2.6 miles, Brasstown Road becomes a dirt road.
GPS coordinates: N34 43.150 / W83 18.104
Maps: *DeLorme: South Carolina Atlas and Gazetteer* page 16, C1
About the campsites: Two primitive campsites sit alongside Brasstown Creek, each requiring a very short hike to reach. The first one sits about 100 feet in, and the next is about 100 yards farther. The creek passes by these primitive campsites, moving slowly at first but swiftly picking up speed as it flows downstream to Brasstown Falls. The sites offer the bare minimum in amenities, with a mere stone fire ring on each. But if you continue hiking past the second campsite, you come upon Brasstown Falls. You're in for a real treat too, since Brasstown Creek actually has three waterfalls: Upper, Middle, and Lower. Each of the three have a unique beauty unto itself. The good news? You get to sleep to the sound of the creek rushing by. The bad news? This is a fairly popular trail, so you also have a bit of foot traffic passing by throughout the day en route to view the Brasstown beauties. To find your way to the many more fantastic waterfalls that this area has to offer, pick up a copy of *FalconGuides: Hiking Waterfalls in Georgia and South Carolina* and continue to explore.

76 Woodall Shoals Primitive Campsites

Location: About 15 miles northwest of Westminster
Season: Year-round
Sites: 4
Maximum length: n/a
Facilities: Vault toilet, fire rings, picnic table (at 1 site only), pet friendly
Fee per night: None
Management: Sumter National Forest–Andrew Pickens District
Contact: (864) 638-9568; www.fs.usda.gov/recarea/scnfs/recreation/camping-cabins/recarea/?recid=47125&actid=29
Finding the campsites: From the junction of US 76 and SC 123 in Westminster, drive west on US 76 for 14.9 miles to a left onto Orchard Road (SR 538) and travel for 0.3 mile to a right onto unmarked FR 757. Follow FR 757 for 2.2 miles to the end.

From the junction of US 76 and the South Carolina/Georgia state line, drive east on US 76 for 2.3 miles to a right onto Orchard Road (SR 538) and follow directions above.
Note: FR 757 is unmarked, and gravel, with a 0.1-mile paved portion halfway to Woodall Shoals.

Llamas sure do make some funny faces.

GPS coordinates: N34 47.880 / W83 18.694

Maps: *DeLorme: South Carolina Atlas and Gazetteer* page 16, B1

About the campsites: Four designated campsites can be found west of the parking lot, along the trail near Woodall Shoals. Woodall Shoals is a class VI rapid found along section IV of the Wild and Scenic Chattooga River and is touted as the most dangerous rapid on the river. A short trail of less than 0.25 mile leads from the parking area to the river. From here, you can enjoy a picnic as you watch the whitewater rafters paddle by, bypassing the treacherous rapid. You can fish from the banks if you have a South Carolina state fishing license, or explore on one of the many hiking or bridle trails in the area. Camping is prohibited in the parking lot and on the beach along the river.

77 Thrifts Ferry Primitive Campsite

Location: About 15 miles northwest of Westminster

Season: Year-round

Sites: 2

Maximum length: n/a

Facilities: Primitive fire rings, pet friendly

Fee per night: None

Management: Sumter National Forest–Andrew Pickens District

Contact: (864) 638-9568; www.fs.usda.gov/recarea/scnfs/recreation/camping-cabins/recarea/?recid=47121&actid=29

Finding the campsite: From the junction of US 76 and SC 183 in Westminster, drive west on US 76 for 16.2 miles to a right onto Thrifts Ferry Road (FR 795). Travel for 0.1 mile to a hard left onto a narrow dirt road that leads from the first campsite to the second campsite at the end of the road.

From the junction of US 76 and the South Carolina/Georgia state line, drive east on US 76 for just over 1.0 mile to a left onto Thrifts Ferry Road (FR 795) and follow the directions above.

GPS coordinates: N34 48.785 / W83 17.349

Maps: *DeLorme: South Carolina Atlas and Gazetteer* page 16, B1

About the campsite: The campsites at Thrifts Ferry are right off US 76. As a matter of fact, you can even see the road from the second campsite. The only amenity at either site is a stone fire ring with a log or two to sit upon, and that's all. The sites are obviously not very deep into the forest, and you can hear the traffic as it passes by. The main reason anyone would choose this location is that it's easy to reach, and that there's a Chattooga River access area just west of Thrifts Ferry off US 76. Kayakers and whitewater rafters use this launch site on a daily basis. If you find these campsites are full, head down the road to Woodall Shoals. It's just as primitive but has about four campsites to pitch a tent on rather than two.

78 Double Branch Primitive Campsite

Location: About 10 miles west of Walhalla
Season: Year-round
Sites: 1
Maximum length: n/a
Facilities: Primitive fire ring, pet friendly
Fee per night: None
Management: Sumter National Forest–Andrew Pickens District
Contact: (864) 638-9568; www.fs.usda.gov/recarea/scnfs/recreation/camping-cabins/recarea/?recid=47083&actid=29
Finding the campsite: From the junction of SC 28 and SC 183 in Walhalla, drive north on SC 28 for 6.1 miles to a left onto Whetstone Road. Follow Whetstone Road for 0.7 mile to a left onto Cassidy Bridge Road and travel for 6.7 miles to a left onto Double Branch Road (FR 742). Follow Double Branch Road for 1.5 miles to a small dirt road that heads northeast uphill to the campsite.

From the junction of SC 28 and SC 107 near Mountain Rest, drive south on SC 28 for 1.9 miles to a right onto Whetstone Road and follow the directions above.
GPS coordinates: N34 46.541 / W83 13.504
Maps: *DeLorme: South Carolina Atlas and Gazetteer* page 22, A1
About the campsite: This single primitive campsite sits atop a small knoll and well off the beaten path in the Andrew Pickens district of the Sumter National Forest. Birds sing throughout the day in your home away from home, and you can get a glimpse of the Chauga River resting far below. A hiking trail leads from the campsite down to the river, and miles of hiking, mountain bike, and bridle trails can be found throughout this region of the forest. If you're looking for something out of the ordinary to do on your visit, check out Wildwater outfitters off Academy Road. They have zip lines on the property and offer whitewater rafting trips on several local area rivers. For more information or to book your adventure, check out their website at www.wildwaterrafting.com.

79 Cassidy Bridge Hunt Camp

Location: About 10 miles west of Walhalla
Season: Year-round
Sites: 1 site can accommodate up to 100 people, although individual/family campers can use the site when it is not reserved
Maximum length: None
Facilities: Vault toilets, one lantern holder, pet friendly
Fee per night: $–$$$
Management: Sumter National Forest–Andrew Pickens District
Contact: (864) 638-9568; www.fs.usda.gov/recarea/scnfs/recreation/camping-cabins/recarea/?recid=47067&actid=29; for reservations, call (877) 444-6777 or visit www.recreation.gov.
Finding the campground: From the junction of SC 28 and SC 183 in Walhalla, drive north on SC 28 for 6.1 miles to a left onto Whetstone Road (SR 193). Follow Whetstone Road for 0.7 mile to

An old hand water pump supplies campers with water.

a left onto Cassidy Bridge Road (SR 290) and travel for 4.6 miles to a left onto FR 745. Follow FR 745 for 0.5 mile to the campground at the end of the road.

From the junction of SC 28 and SC 107 near Mountain Rest, drive south on SC 28 for 1.9 miles to a right onto Whetstone Road and follow the directions above.

GPS coordinates: N34 47.156 / W83 12.567

Maps: *DeLorme: South Carolina Atlas and Gazetteer* page 22, A1

About the campground: This primitive hunt camp sits right along the edge of the Chauga River. It was designed as a group camp, but when it's not reserved, individuals and families can also camp here. Groups of up to 100 people are welcome, and while you can hear the river running by, the lay of the land really only allows for a few tents to be pitched near the water's edge. The river is heavy with fish, and the area is quite popular with the local anglers. But be sure you have a South Carolina state fishing license before you cast your line. There are ample outdoor opportunities to explore the surrounding Sumter National Forest by foot or on horseback. Or visit one of the local river raft outfitters nearby, and try your hand at some whitewater rafting while you're here. As a matter of fact, the Wildwater outfitters property is just a few miles away off Academy Road, and they also offer zip line canopy tours. When planning your trip, check out their website at www.wildwaterrafting.com. If you notice the sound of frequent gunshots in the distance, don't be concerned. The Cedar Creek Rifle Range is just up the road less than 2 miles away. Campers must make reservations in advance. The campsite has a locked gate, and the forest service will disclose the gate code when you make your reservation. Fees vary throughout the year; for more information, contact the US Forest Service directly.

80 Fall Creek Primitive Campsite

Location: About 16 miles northwest of Westminster
Season: Year-round
Sites: 1
Maximum length: n/a
Facilities: None, pet friendly
Fee per night: None
Management: Sumter National Forest–Andrew Pickens District
Contact: (864) 638-9568; www.fs.usda.gov/recarea/scnfs/recreation/camping-cabins/recarea/?recid=47123&actid=29
Finding the campsite: From the junction of US 76 and SC 123 in Westminster, drive west on US 76 for 15.2 miles to a right onto Chattooga Ridge Road and travel for 2.0 miles to a left onto Fall Creek Road. Follow Fall Creek Road for 0.3 mile to a left onto FR 722 (Fall Creek Road Extension) and travel for 2.0 miles to a left onto FR 769. Follow FR 769 for 0.5 mile to the campsite on the left before the loop at the end of the road.

From the junction of US 76 and the Chattooga River Bridge (South Carolina/Georgia state line), drive east on US 76 for 2.0 miles to a left onto Chattooga Ridge Road and follow the directions above.

From the junction of SC 28 and SC 183 in Walhalla, drive north on SC 28 for 6.1 miles to a left onto Whetstone Road. Follow Whetstone Road for approximately 6.0 miles to a left onto Chattooga Ridge Road. Travel for 3.8 miles to a right onto Fall Creek Road and follow the directions above.

A short hike leads to Fall Creek Falls.

From the junction of SC 28 and SC 107 near Mountain Rest, drive south on SC 28 for 1.9 miles to a right onto Whetstone Road, and follow the directions above.

GPS coordinates: N34 49.927 / W83 15.714

Maps: *DeLorme: South Carolina Atlas and Gazetteer* page 16, H1

About the campsite: A large open area with an obvious place to build a campfire comprises the single primitive campsite at Fall Creek. Although the campsite is not actually on Fall Creek, a short, moderate, 0.1-mile hike leads you to the base of Fall Creek Falls. I highly recommend that you take the time to visit the falls while you're in the area. And if you'd like to see several more waterfalls nearby, grab a copy of *Hiking Waterfalls in Georgia and South Carolina* before you come. It will guide you to the area's many wonderful waterfalls. For those adrenaline junkies in the crowd, head over to the Nantahala Outdoor Center's (NOC) Chattooga River Outpost off Chattooga Ridge Road. They offer some of the area's most premier whitewater rafting opportunities on the famous Wild and Scenic Chattooga River. For more information or to book your reservation, check out their website at www.noc.com. If you find that the Fall Creek campsite is occupied upon your arrival, head just a tad bit farther up the road to Turpin Branch.

81 Turpin Branch Primitive Campsite

Location: About 16 miles northwest of Westminster

Season: Year-round

Sites: 1

Maximum length: n/a

Facilities: Primitive fire ring, pet friendly

Fee per night: None

Management: Sumter National Forest–Andrew Pickens District

Contact: (864) 638-9568; www.fs.usda.gov/recarea/scnfs/recreation/camping-cabins/recarea/?recid=47119&actid=29

Finding the campsite: From the junction of US 76 and SC 123 in Westminster, drive west on US 76 for 15.2 miles to a right onto Chattooga Ridge Road and travel for 2.0 miles to a left onto Fall Creek Road. Follow Fall Creek Road for 0.3 mile to a left onto FR 722 (Fall Creek Road Extension) and travel for 2.0 miles to FR 769 on your left. Continue to follow FR 722 past FR 769 for 100 yards to the campsite on the right.

From the junction of US 76 and the Chattooga River Bridge (South Carolina/Georgia state line), drive east on US 76 for 2.0 miles to a left onto Chattooga Ridge Road and follow the directions above.

From the junction of SC 28 and SC 183 in Walhalla, drive north on SC 28 for 6.1 miles to a left onto Whetstone Road. Follow Whetstone Road for approximately 6.0 miles to a left onto Chattooga Ridge Road. Travel for 3.8 miles to a right onto Fall Creek Road and follow the directions above.

From the junction of SC 28 and SC 107 near Mountain Rest, drive south on SC 28 for 1.9 miles to a right onto Whetstone Road and follow the directions above.

GPS coordinates: N34 50.007 / W83 15.184

Maps: *DeLorme: South Carolina Atlas and Gazetteer* page 16, H1

About the campsite: A short, muddy dirt road leads back to this primitive campsite, but it may be impassable at times without a high clearance vehicle. As is typical with the Sumter National Forest primitive campsites in this region, the campsite has the bare minimum. A single stone fire ring and a flat area to pitch a few tents is it. If Turpin Branch is occupied, you can camp at the Fall Creek campsite. And while you're in the area, I highly recommend a quick hike to Fall Creek Falls, whose trailhead is off FR 769. For specific directions to this and many other waterfalls in the area, pick up a copy of *Hiking Waterfalls in Georgia and South Carolina*. You won't be disappointed. If you are looking for something a little more high energy, check out the Nantahala Outdoor Center's (NOC) Chattooga River Outpost off Chattooga Ridge Road. They offer thrilling whitewater rafting opportunities on the famous Wild and Scenic Chattooga River. Portions of the movie *Deliverance* were filmed on the Chattooga, and the river boasts class V and VI rapids. For more information or to book your reservation, check out their website at www.noc.com.

82 Grapevine Primitive Campground

Location: About 13 miles northwest of Westminster
Season: Year-round
Sites: 15
Maximum Length: n/a
Facilities: Vault toilets, fire rings, lantern holders, pet friendly
Fee per night: None
Management: Sumter National Forest–Andrew Pickens District
Contact: (864) 638-9568; www.fs.usda.gov/recarea/scnfs/recreation/camping-cabins/recarea/?recid=47097&actid=29
Finding the campground: From the junction of SC 28 and SC 183 in Walhalla, drive north on SC 28 for 6.1 miles to a left onto Whetstone Road. Follow Whetstone Road for approximately 6.0 miles to a left onto Chattooga Ridge Road. Travel for 1.6 miles to a left onto Grapevine Branch Road (FR 764) and drive for 2.4 miles to the campground at the end of the road.

From the junction of SC 28 and SC 107 near Mountain Rest, drive south on SC 28 for 1.9 miles to a right onto Whetstone Road, and follow the directions above.

From the junction of US 76 and SC 123 in Westminster, drive west on US 76 for 15.2 miles to a right onto Chattooga Ridge Road and travel for 4.2 miles to a right onto Grapevine Branch Road. Follow Grapevine Branch Road for 2.4 miles to the campground at the end of the road.

From the junction of US 76 and the Chattooga River Bridge (South Carolina/Georgia state line), drive east on US 76 for 2.0 miles to a left onto Chattooga Ridge Road and follow the directions above.

GPS coordinates: N34 49.388 / W83 10.855
Maps: *DeLorme: South Carolina Atlas and Gazetteer* page 16, H2
About the campground: This busy campground can be found along a narrow stretch of the Chauga River and even has a wheelchair-accessible campsite. Which is quite surprising considering the primitive nature of the remaining campsites. There are no markings to differentiate one campsite from the next, and the only amenities on-site are fire rings, an occasional lantern holder, and a vault toilet. Be sure to arrive early if you hope to secure a good spot, as the steady stream of the rocky river makes this a prime location. Not to mention, the price is certainly right. Locals

Waterwheels once powered many mills in the area.

frequent this campground weekend after weekend, keeping it occupied throughout the year. Unfortunately, these same locals tend to take it for granted, and the campground is often littered with trash come Monday morning. Please remember to respect Mother Nature and others as well. Pick up after yourself, keep a clean camp, and most importantly, pack it in, pack it out.

83 Blackwell Bridge Primitive Campsite

Location: On the north side of Whetstone Road by the Chauga River Bridge; about 7 miles northwest of Walhalla, and about 3 miles southwest of Mountain Rest
Season: Year-round
Sites: 1
Maximum length: n/a
Facilities: Primitive fire rings, pet friendly
Fee per night: None
Management: Sumter National Forest–Andrew Pickens District

I always wondered who lived in those holes.

Contact: (864) 638-9568; www.fs.usda.gov/recarea/scnfs/recreation/camping-cabins/recarea/?recid=47075&actid=29

Finding the campsite: From the junction of SC 28 and SC 183 in Walhalla, drive north on SC 28 for 6.1 miles to a left onto Whetstone Road. Follow Whetstone Road for 5.0 miles to the campsite on the right just after crossing the bridge over the Chauga River.

From the junction of SC 28 and SC 107 near Mountain Rest, drive south on SC 28 for 1.9 miles to a right onto Whetstone Road, and follow the directions above.

From the junction of US 76 and SC 123 in Westminster, drive west on US 76 for 15.2 miles to a right onto Chattooga Ridge Road and travel for 5.7 miles to a stop sign at Whetstone Road. Go right, and follow Whetstone Road for 1.0 mile to the campsite on the left just before crossing the bridge over the Chauga River.

From the junction of US 76 and the Chattooga River Bridge (South Carolina/Georgia state line), drive east on US 76 for 2.0 miles to a left onto Chattooga Ridge Road and follow the directions above.

GPS coordinates: N34 50.031 / W83 10.513

Maps: *DeLorme: South Carolina Atlas and Gazetteer* page 16, H2

About the campsite: If you have a regular passenger car, I recommend that you park at the beginning of FR 734 and hike down the bumpy road to the campsite. But if you have an SUV or a high clearance vehicle, you can drive the 0.1 mile on FR 734 to the end of the road. The Blackwell Bridge campsite, named for the old bridge whose remains you can see on the south side of Whetstone Road, sits right along the banks of the Chauga River. A perfect location for dipping your feet in the water, or trying your hand at fishing, but you must have a South Carolina fishing license with you. The sound of the river rushing by pacifies you as you head off to sleep, but unfortunately, the campsite is right next to the road as well, so you also hear the occasional car passing by. The campsite has a primitive fire ring, and no bathrooms, so please respect Mother Nature and others who may camp here in the future. Remember all cat holes must be dug at least 200 feet from the river.

84 Whetstone Horse Camp

Location: Near the end of Whetstone Road (FR 721); about 7 miles northwest of Walhalla, and about 3 miles southwest of Mountain Rest

Season: Year-round

Sites: 18

Maximum length: None

Facilities: Vault toilets, water spigots dispersed, fire rings, picnic tables, lantern holders, pet friendly

Fee per night: $$

Management: Sumter National Forest–Andrew Pickens District

Contact: (864) 638-9568; www.fs.usda.gov/recarea/scnfs/recreation/camping-cabins/recarea/?recid=47071&actid=29; for reservations, call (877) 444-6777 or visit www.recreation.gov

Finding the campground: From the junction of SC 28 and SC 183 in Walhalla, drive north on SC 28 for 6.1 miles to a left onto Whetstone Road. Follow Whetstone Road for approximately 6.0 miles to a stop sign. Continue straight ahead for another 2.7 miles to the campground on the left.

From the junction of SC 28 and SC 107 near Mountain Rest, drive south on SC 28 for 1.9 miles to a right onto Whetstone Road, and follow the directions above.

Whetstone offers superb horse camping.

From the junction of US 76 and SC 123 in Westminster, drive west on US 76 for 15.2 miles to a right onto Chattooga Ridge Road and travel for 5.7 miles to a stop sign at Whetstone Road. Go left, and follow Whetstone Road (FR 721) for 2.7 miles to the campground on the left.

From the junction of US 76 and the Chattooga River Bridge (South Carolina/Georgia state line), drive east on US 76 for 2.0 miles to a left onto Chattooga Ridge Road and follow the directions above.

GPS coordinates: N34 51.713 / W83 13.448

Maps: *DeLorme: South Carolina Atlas and Gazetteer* page 16, H1

About the campground: Horse tethers and ample parking for your trailer are just the beginning at this equestrian lover's dream. With manure bins on-site, and a "ride-in/ride-out" location, this is the best horse camp I've seen in the region. The Rocky Gap bridle trail can be accessed directly from the campground. Hikers are also welcome to use the trail, and after a long day in the forest, clean, deep, well-groomed campsites are a welcome sight. Whetstone is not only wonderful for horse camping, but its proximity to Earl's Ford River access makes it ideal for kayakers as well. Earl's Ford is a popular access point for the Wild and Scenic Chattooga River and is located just over a mile up the road at the end of FR 721.

85 Timmy Place Primitive Campsite

Location: About 16 miles northwest of Westminster
Season: Year-round
Sites: 1
Maximum length: n/a
Facilities: Primitive fire ring, pet friendly
Fee per night: None
Management: Sumter National Forest–Andrew Pickens District
Contact: (864) 638-9568; www.fs.usda.gov/recarea/scnfs/recreation/camping-cabins/recarea/?recid=47167&actid=29
Finding the campsite: From the junction of SC 28 and SC 183 in Walhalla, drive north on SC 28 for 6.1 miles to a left onto Whetstone Road. Follow Whetstone Road for approximately 6.0 miles to a stop sign. Continue straight ahead for another 3.7 miles to a left into the overflow parking area just before reaching the Earl's Ford River Access Area. Follow this dirt road through the parking areas for 0.1 mile to the campsite at the end of the road.

A bumblebee searches for sweet nectar in these rhododendron flowers.

From the junction of SC 28 and SC 107 near Mountain Rest, drive south on SC 28 for 1.9 miles to a right onto Whetstone Road, and follow the directions above.

From the junction of US 76 and SC 123 in Westminster, drive west on US 76 for 15.2 miles to a right onto Chattooga Ridge Road and travel for 5.7 miles to a stop sign at Whetstone Road. Go left, and follow Whetstone Road (FR 721) for 3.7 miles to a left into the overflow parking area just before reaching the Earl's Ford River Access Area. Follow this dirt road through the parking areas for 0.1 mile to the campsite at the end of the road.

From the junction of US 76 and the Chattooga River Bridge (South Carolina/Georgia state line), drive east on US 76 for 2.0 miles to a left onto Chattooga Ridge Road and follow the directions above.

GPS coordinates: N34 52.451 / W83 13.756

Maps: *DeLorme: South Carolina Atlas and Gazetteer* page 16, H1

About the campsite: A single primitive campsite where you can see that people have built a fire is all this site has to offer. Earl's Ford is just around the corner, and Timmy Place actually sits at the end of the overflow parking area for it. Kayakers and whitewater rafters use this popular Chattooga River access point throughout the summer, but it's not too often that cars make it all the way back to Timmy Place. In part, because the road leading to the campsite is not well maintained, so you may need a high clearance vehicle to reach it. The Whetstone Horse Campground is just a mile away, so if this is a bit too rustic for you, I suggest you camp there. With miles of hiking and bridle trails near the horse camp, and the Chattooga River within easy reach, this area offers several ways to enjoy the great outdoors.

Walhalla to Mountain Rest Area

Campground	Total sites	Hookup sites	Max. RV length	Hookups	Toilets	Showers	Drinking water	Dump station	Recreation	Fee	Reservations
86 **Long Bottom Ford Primitive Campsites**	6	0	n/a	N	V	N	N	N	H, F, B*, L*	No Fee	N
87 **Nicholson Field Primitive Campsite**	1	0	n/a	N	N	N	N	N	H, F, B*, L*	No Fee	N
88 **Oconee State Park**	155	139	50'	E, W	F	Y	Y	Y	H, M, S, F, B*, BB, MG, G*, V, P	$$-$$$	Y
89 **Tamassee Primitive Campsite**	1	0	n/a	N	N	N	N	N	H, R, F, P	No Fee	N
90 **Cherry Hill Campground**	29	0	40'*	N	F	Y	Y	N	H, F, P	$$	Y
91 **Big Bend Primitive Campsite**	1	0	n/a	N	N	N	N	N	H, F	No Fee	N
92 **King Creek Primitive Campsite**	1	0	n/a	N	N	N	N	N	H, F	No Fee	N
93 **Burrells Ford Backcountry Campground**	16	0	n/a	N	V	N	N	N	H, S, F, P	No Fee	N

* See campground entry for specific information

86 Long Bottom Ford Primitive Campsites

Location: About 12 miles northwest of Walhalla
Season: Year-round
Sites: 6
Maximum length: n/a
Facilities: Vault toilets, primitive fire rings, lantern holders, pet friendly
Fee per night: None
Management: Sumter National Forest–Andrew Pickens District
Contact: (864) 638-9568; www.fs.usda.gov/recarea/scnfs/recreation/camping-cabins/recarea/?recid=47103&actid=29
Finding the campsites: From the junction of SC 28 and SC 107 near Mountain Rest, drive north on SC 28 for approximately 6.5 miles to a left onto Low Water Bridge Road. Follow Low Water Bridge Road for 0.4 mile to the campsites on the left.

From the junction of SC 28 and the South Carolina/Georgia state line near Satolah, drive south on SC 28 for approximately 1.8 miles to a right onto Low Water Bridge Road and follow the directions above.
GPS coordinates: N34 54.069 / W83 11.051
Maps: *DeLorme: South Carolina Atlas and Gazetteer* page 16, G2

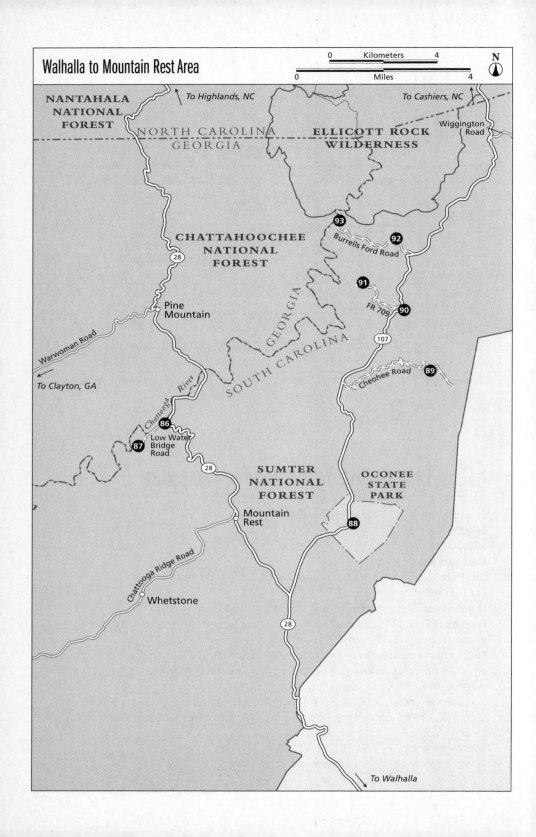

Walhalla to Mountain Rest Area

NANTAHALA
NATIONAL
FOREST

To Highlands, NC

To Cashiers, NC

NORTH CAROLINA
GEORGIA

ELLICOTT ROCK
WILDERNESS

Wiggington
Road

CHATTAHOOCHEE
NATIONAL
FOREST

93

92

Burrells Ford Road

28

91

FR 709

90

Pine
Mountain

107

GEORGIA

SOUTH CAROLINA

Cheohee Road

89

Warwoman Road

Chattooga River

To Clayton, GA

86

87

Low Water
Bridge
Road

28

SUMTER
NATIONAL
FOREST

OCONEE
STATE
PARK

Mountain
Rest

88

Chattooga Ridge Road

28

Whetstone

28

To Walhalla

This fluffy sheep has yet to be sheared.

About the campsites: Although the national forest website has this listed as a single primitive campsite, in reality, several campsites line the dirt road just across from the Wild and Scenic Chattooga River. A lantern holder and stone fire rings comprise each campsite, and there's room to pitch a few tents on most. A river access point can be found just before reaching the "campground," which is one reason the sites stay surprisingly busy. Be sure to register your float plan prior to launching your canoe or kayak.

87 Nicholson Field Primitive Campsite

Location: About 12 miles northwest of Walhalla
Season: Year-round
Sites: 1
Maximum length: n/a
Facilities: Primitive fire ring, pet friendly
Fee per night: None
Management: Sumter National Forest–Andrew Pickens District
Contact: (864) 638-9568; www.fs.usda.gov/recarea/scnfs/recreation/camping-cabins/recarea/?recid=70864&actid=29
Finding the campsite: From the junction of SC 28 and SC 107 near Mountain Rest, drive north on SC 28 for approximately 6.5 miles to a left onto Low Water Bridge Road. Follow Low Water

Bridge Road for 1.1 miles to a three-way fork. Take the middle fork straight ahead, and follow FR 779 for 0.1 mile to the campsite at the end of the road.

From the junction of SC 28 and the South Carolina/North Carolina state line near Satolah, drive south on SC 28 for 1.8 miles to a right onto Low Water Bridge Road and follow the directions above.

GPS coordinates: N34 53.482 / W83 11.655

Maps: *DeLorme: South Carolina Atlas and Gazetteer* page 16, G2

About the campsite: A large, flat open area at the end of the road, with plenty of parking, and a primitive fire ring, is all that greets you at Nicholson Field. The National Forest Service website actually has this listed as a campground, and Long Bottom Ford listed as a primitive campsite, but in fact, it's the other way around. Although it's very primitive, this prime location near the Wild and Scenic Chattooga River makes this a good spot to gather with friends, especially if you are river rafters or whitewater kayakers. There's a river access point less than a mile down Low Water Bridge Road, but be sure to register before you push off. You can fish from the banks of the river, but you must obtain a South Carolina state fishing license before you bait your hook and cast your line. Be forewarned, a high clearance vehicle may be necessary prior to heading down FR 779. If you don't have one, park off to the side of the road and haul your belongings the last 0.1 mile on foot. Another option is to simply stay just up the road at Long Bottom Ford.

88 Oconee State Park

Location: 624 State Park Rd., Mountain Rest; about 12 miles north of Walhalla, and about 18 miles south of Cashiers, North Carolina

Season: Year-round

Sites: 154; 1 group camp area is also available and can accommodate up to 50 people; cabin rentals are also available

Maximum length: 50 feet

Facilities: Flush toilets, hot showers, electric, water, fire rings, picnic tables, dump station, ice and firewood for sale, pet friendly

Fee per night: $$–$$$

Management: South Carolina Department of Natural Resources

Contact: (864) 638-5353; www.southcarolinaparks.com/oconee/camping.aspx; for reservations call (866) 345-7275 or visit www.reserveamerica.com

Finding the campground: From the junction of SC 107 and SC 28 near Mountain Rest, drive north on SC 107 for 2.4 miles to the entrance to the park on the right.

From the junction of SC 107 and Wiggington Road (SR 413), drive south on SC 107 for 11.4 miles to the entrance to the park on the left.

GPS coordinates: N34 52.032 / W83 06.436

Maps: *DeLorme: South Carolina Atlas and Gazetteer* page 16, H3

About the campground: Oconee State Park is quite lovely and was one of the original parks developed by the Civilian Conservation Corps back in the 1930s. The park is full of activities and even has a small putt-putt golf course. As for the camping, it's a mixed bag. One loop sits above the lake, with gravel sites fairly close to one another giving you little privacy. The next loop is a bit more wooded and better spaced, while a third has paved campsites that are right on top of each

An old gas pump is on display at Oconee State Park.

other, much like an RV park. So you need to choose your site wisely and may even want to take a drive through the park before committing to a campsite. A separate tent camping area requires a short walk but offers a lot more privacy than the main body of the campground. There are laundry facilities on-site, which is great for extended stays. Plus, there's something to do for everyone in the family. They have a swim area, a fishing pier, boat rentals (no private boats are allowed on park lakes), volleyball, basketball, and open fields to play in. The park has hiking trails that can also be used by mountain bikers, and one trail even leads 2.4 miles to the 60-foot Hidden Falls. The area surrounding the park is laden with trails galore, including the famous Foothills Trail, and many of the Upcountry's other waterfalls are within easy reach. To find them with ease, check out *Hiking Waterfalls in Georgia and South Carolina*. For a very unique experience, while you're in the area, take a drive south on SC 28 and visit the Stumphouse Tunnel. It's a one of a kind.

89 Tamassee Primitive Campsite

Location: About 16 miles north of Walhalla, and about 17 miles south of Cashiers, North Carolina
Season: Year-round
Sites: 1
Maximum length: n/a
Facilities: Primitive fire ring, pet friendly
Fee per night: None
Management: Sumter National Forest–Andrew Pickens District
Contact: (864) 638-9568; www.fs.usda.gov/recarea/scnfs/recreation/camping-cabins/recarea/?recid=47115&actid=29
Finding the campsite: From the junction of SC 107 and SC 28 near Mountain Rest, drive north on SC 107 for 6.2 miles to a right onto Cheohee Road (FR 710, aka Winding Stairs Road) and travel for 3.4 miles to the campsite on the right, just after crossing two small creeks.

From the junction of SC 107 and Wiggington Road (SR 413), drive south on SC 107 for 7.6 miles to a left onto Cheohee Road (FR 710, aka Winding Stairs Road) and follow the directions above.
GPS coordinates: N34 55.320 / W83 04.642
Maps: *DeLorme: South Carolina Atlas and Gazetteer* page 16, G3
About the campsite: The Foothills Trail runs through the forest nearby, and Townes Creek flows right by this wide-open camping area. Although it's listed with the US Forest Service as a single campsite, there's easily enough room to pitch several tents. The constant and tranquil sound of the creek can be heard throughout the night, lulling you to sleep. There are no amenities except for a few man-made fire rings, but this is one of the few places in the region that allows pack animals, so feel free to bring your horse along. This creek-side campsite is quite lovely, but unfortunately, the area is frequented by people who like to leave their trash behind, littering the area. Please remember, whether you're here or at any campsite, to practice leave no trace camping and pack it in, pack it out. No one wants to arrive at a campsite full of trash. A little plain and simple courtesy goes a long way.

90 Cherry Hill Campground

Location: About 16 miles north of Walhalla, and about 14 miles south of Cashiers, North Carolina
Season: April–October
Sites: 29
Maximum length: 40 feet, but there are a limited number of sites that can accommodate this size RV
Facilities: Flush toilets, hot showers, water spigots dispersed, fire rings, picnic tables, lantern holders, dump station, pet friendly
Fee per night: $$
Management: Sumter National Forest–Andrew Pickens District
Contact: (864) 638-9568; www.fs.usda.gov/recarea/scnfs/recreation/camping-cabins/recarea/?recid=47069&actid=31; for reservations, call (877) 444-6777 or visit www.recreation.gov
Finding the campground: From the junction of SC 107 and SC 28 near Mountain Rest, drive north on SC 107 for 8.6 miles to a right onto Cherry Hill Rec. Road (FR 735) at the entrance to the campground.

A wild turkey tom struts his stuff.

From the junction of SC 107 and Wiggington Road (SR 413), drive south on SC 107 for 5.2 miles to the campground on the right. **Note:** When driving north on SC 107, be sure to pass Cherry Hill Road on your right, and continue to drive north to a right onto Cherry Hill Rec. Road.

GPS coordinates: N34 55.320 / W83 04.642

Maps: *DeLorme: South Carolina Atlas and Gazetteer* page 16, F3

About the campground: Cherry Hill can be found just south of the North Carolina state line and just east of the Chattooga River. Nicely spaced, wooded campsites welcome you with open arms. Some of the sites even sit alongside a small brook. The campground is popular with hunters, since it offers more amenities than most hunt camps, and the surrounding area offers plenty to do. Fish in one of the many creeks, rivers, or lakes, explore the hiking trails within the nearby Ellicott Rock Wilderness, or head out to one of many wonderful waterfalls in the area. *Hiking Waterfalls in Georgia and South Carolina* is a great tool to help you find them. For something fun and different, you can head up the road to the Walhalla Fish Hatchery or enjoy a picnic in the Chattooga Picnic Area. If you feel the need for a bit of civilization, you're within easy reach of Walhalla to the south, and Cashiers, North Carolina, to the north. I must address one important issue in regards to access to Cherry Hill Campground. FR 735 is narrow, and trees hang overhead. Even though a few of the campsites can fit RVs as big as 40 feet, you must be a good driver to maneuver into these sites. If you're not comfortable with that, or if you have a big rig, I recommend you head down the road to Oconee State Park where they can fit RVs as large as 50 feet comfortably. Smaller campers, pop-ups, and tent campers will have no problems enjoying the pleasantly wooded atmosphere at Cherry Hill Campground.

91 Big Bend Primitive Campsite

Location: About 15 miles north of Walhalla, and about 15 miles south of Cashiers, North Carolina

Season: Year-round

Sites: 1

Maximum length: n/a

Facilities: Primitive fire ring, pet friendly

Fee per night: None

Management: Sumter National Forest–Andrew Pickens District

Contact: (864) 638-9568; www.fs.usda.gov/recarea/scnfs/recreation/camping-cabins/recarea/?recid=47073&actid=29

Finding the campsite: From the junction of SC 107 and SC 28 near Mountain Rest, drive north on SC 107 for 8.6 miles to a right onto FR 709 (across from Cherry Hill Campground). Follow FR 709 for 1.7 miles to the end at the campsite. **Note:** FR 709 is a rough, narrow, bumpy forest service road and may require a high clearance vehicle.

From the junction of SC 107 and Wiggington Road (SR 413), drive south on SC 107 for 5.2 miles to a left onto FR 709 (across from Cherry Hill Campground) and follow the directions above.

GPS coordinates: N34 56.990 / W83 06.420

Maps: *DeLorme: South Carolina Atlas and Gazetteer* page 16, F3

About the campsite: A single campsite sits atop a small knoll at the end of the bumpy forest service road. There's a nicely stacked stone fire ring and some hay laid out as a tent pad. But don't expect any other luxuries at Big Bend. A hiking trail leads from the campsite down to the Wild and Scenic Chattooga River, where you can try your hand at fishing, provided you have a South Carolina state fishing license with you. If you're lucky, you may see some whitewater rafters or kayakers as they paddle by. You can also access the Chattooga Trail and the Foothills Trail from the campsite. But be sure you bring a good topographical map and a compass along before heading out to explore.

92 King Creek Primitive Campsite

Location: About 18 miles north of Walhalla, and about 12 miles south of Cashiers, North Carolina
Season: Year-round
Sites: 1
Maximum length: n/a
Facilities: Primitive fire ring, pet friendly
Fee per night: None
Management: Sumter National Forest–Andrew Pickens District

This cute little baby goat found an odd place to lounge about.

Contact: (864) 638-9568; www.fs.usda.gov/recarea/scnfs/recreation/camping-cabins/recarea/?recid=47077&actid=29

Finding the campsite: From the junction of SC 107 and SC 28 near Mountain Rest, drive north on SC 107 for 10.0 miles to a left onto unmarked Burrells Ford Road. Follow Burrells Ford Road for 0.6 mile to a hard right onto the narrow dirt road FR 708C, and travel for 0.1 mile to the campsite at the end of the road.

From the junction of SC 107 and Wiggington Road (SR 413), drive south on SC 107 for 3.8 miles to a right onto unmarked Burrells Ford Road and follow the directions above.

Note: FR 708C may be overgrown and impassable at times.

GPS coordinates: N34 57.931 / W83 05.475

Maps: *DeLorme: South Carolina Atlas and Gazetteer* page 16, F3

About the campsite: Lush green grass with a fire ring in the middle is all that comprises the King Creek campsite. The site sits right beside King Creek, a tributary of the Wild and Scenic Chattooga River. You can fish from your campsite, but be sure you know the limits, and that you have a South Carolina state fishing license before you cast your line. King Creek Falls is just down the road, and is accessed from the Burrells Ford parking area. Several other waterfalls are within easy reach as well. I highly recommend *Hiking Waterfalls in Georgia and South Carolina* to help you find them. Note, the road leading down to the campsite is quite narrow and bumpy, and may be impassable at times.

93 Burrells Ford Backcountry Campground

Location: About 18 miles north of Walhalla, and about 12 miles south of Cashiers, North Carolina

Season: Year-round

Sites: 16

Maximum length: n/a

Facilities: Vault toilets, no water, fire rings, picnic tables, lantern holders, bear wires to hang your food, pet friendly

Fee per night: None

Management: Sumter National Forest–Andrew Pickens District

Contact: (864) 638-9568; www.fs.usda.gov/recarea/scnfs/recreation/camping-cabins/recarea/?recid=47065&actid=29

Finding the campground: From the junction of SC 107 and SC 28 near Mountain Rest, drive north on SC 107 for 10.0 miles to a left onto unmarked Burrells Ford Road. Follow Burrells Ford Road for 2.2 miles to the parking area for the campground. The campground requires an easy 0.25-mile hike in.

From the junction of SC 107 and Wiggington Road (SR 413), drive south on SC 107 for 3.8 miles to a right onto unmarked Burrells Ford Road and follow the directions above.

GPS coordinates: N34 58.299 / W83 06.896

Maps: *DeLorme–South Carolina Atlas and Gazetteer* page 16, F3

About the campground: A 0.25-mile hike leads westerly down the wide gravel "road" to the campground. Once you arrive, you find over a dozen crisp, clean campsites all within earshot of the Wild and Scenic Chattooga River. Most of the sites are just far enough apart to give you some privacy. Each has a tent pad and the typical amenities, but they also provide bear-proof bars to hang your

The half-moon brightly shines through the trees.

food from. This is an added plus, since Burrells Ford sits in the middle of black bear country. While the bars are easily accessible, you still need to bring at least 30 feet of rope to string your food up. Also, there is no potable water on-site, so be sure to bring plenty along. A short walk leads to the river, where you can take a dip at your own risk, or try your hand at fly fishing, provided you obtain a South Carolina state fishing license. If you prefer to head deeper into the forest, a 0.5-mile hike leads from the campground to King Creek Falls, a 60-foot waterfall that towers proudly overhead. For specific trail directions to this and many other beautiful waterfalls in the area, pick up a copy of *Hiking Waterfalls in Georgia and South Carolina*. It's an invaluable guide to one of the area's most popular attractions. Although you may have the campground to yourself, you are likely to have hikers passing by on their way to see the falls. But this occasional foot traffic is not enough to deter me from putting Burrells Ford on the Author's Favorites list.

Appendix: Packing List

Who hasn't been there? You leave home, drive a considerable distance to your camp-site, then realize you've left some essential piece of equipment at home. It might be your raincoat or your camp axe or a lighter for the stove and lanterns. Whatever it is, it's something you need and can't get readily.

To avoid that kind of frustration, print a copy of the following and keep it in your camping bin or tote. You might want more than is listed here or less, depending on how you travel. But whenever you are planning to leave home, pull it out and check off items as you pack them in your vehicle. That won't necessarily guarantee you'll always have everything you need on hand, but it helps.

Your list should include:

❏ Reservation paperwork. If you called ahead or reserved space online, take your receipt or confirmation with you.

❏ Backpack, daypack, and/or fanny pack

❏ Bags (grocery bags, always handy for holding odds and ends)

❏ Ice chest with ice

❏ Lantern (with propane, liquid fuel, or batteries, as appropriate, and some extra mantles)

❏ Flashlights or headlamps, with batteries and spare bulbs

❏ Matches, preferably waterproof, and/or a lighter

❏ Tent

❏ Tent rain tarp

❏ Extra tent stakes

❏ Dining fly

❏ Plastic ground cloth for under the tent

❏ Sleeping bag

❏ Sleeping mattress or pad (along with a method of inflating it)

❏ Pillow

❏ Space blanket

❏ Sunscreen

❏ Insect repellent

❏ Poison ivy block

❏ Poison ivy remedies

❏ Allergy medicines

❏ Pain relief pills, like aspirin or acetaminophen

❏ Stomach medicines (for diarrhea, upset stomach, etc.)

- ❏ Tweezers for splinters
- ❏ Antiseptic
- ❏ Band-Aids and bandages
- ❏ Itch cream for bug bites
- ❏ Mole skin to prevent blisters if you hike a lot
- ❏ A first-aid kit that you can take with you on a hike or canoe trip
- ❏ Prescription medicines
- ❏ Extra glasses or contact lenses, and a glasses-repair kit
- ❏ Shower shoes
- ❏ Biodegradable soap
- ❏ Washcloth
- ❏ Bath towel
- ❏ Biodegradable shampoo
- ❏ Biodegradable toothpaste
- ❏ Toothbrush
- ❏ Comb or hair brush
- ❏ Razor and shaving cream
- ❏ Toilet paper (the stuff in state park campgrounds is notoriously cheap, earning more complaints from visitors than just about anything else)
- ❏ A case or bag for carrying everything to the shower house
- ❏ Bathing suit
- ❏ Water shoes
- ❏ Extra dry shoes
- ❏ Sunglasses
- ❏ Axe
- ❏ Bow saw
- ❏ Extension cord for campsites with an electric hookup
- ❏ Duct tape and/or electrical tape
- ❏ Hammer for pounding in tent pegs
- ❏ Rope
- ❏ Clothesline
- ❏ Clothespins
- ❏ Whiskbroom to clean table and tent site
- ❏ Pocket knife
- ❏ Compass and area map
- ❏ Fishing pole, gear, license, and lures or bait

- ❏ Beach chairs
- ❏ Camping chairs
- ❏ Safety pins
- ❏ Cell phone with your car adapter
- ❏ Camera with good batteries
- ❏ Camcorder, also with good batteries and a memory card
- ❏ Money, credit card, and ID (needed to get your senior discount, if nothing else)
- ❏ Books, radio, cards, games, toys, etc.
- ❏ Sports equipment
- ❏ Citronella candles
- ❏ Binoculars
- ❏ Field guides for identifying wildlife
- ❏ Clothing appropriate for the season. Remember, though, that it never hurts to have extra dry socks and an extra sweatshirt or jacket in case the nights get cooler than expected.
- ❏ Wide-brimmed hat to block the sun
- ❏ Jacket
- ❏ Rain gear or poncho (which can double as an emergency lean-to if you're on the trail)
- ❏ Hiking boots
- ❏ Hiking staff
- ❏ Work gloves
- ❏ A few simple tools (pliers, screwdrivers)
- ❏ Stove with fuel and lighter or charcoal and lighter fluid and grill
- ❏ Newspapers or some other tinder for lighting a campfire
- ❏ Firewood
- ❏ Frying pan with lid
- ❏ Cooking skewers for hot dogs, marshmallows, etc.
- ❏ Pot or sauce pan with lid
- ❏ Can opener
- ❏ Tongs
- ❏ Coffeemaker and filters
- ❏ Pot lifter and/or pot holders
- ❏ Tablecloth
- ❏ Plates
- ❏ Mugs/cups
- ❏ Knives, forks, spoons

- ❏ Kitchen knife
- ❏ Mixing bowl
- ❏ Spatula
- ❏ Scrub pad
- ❏ Dish pan for washing dishes
- ❏ Container for water
- ❏ Paper towels and napkins
- ❏ Trash bags
- ❏ Aluminum foil
- ❏ Biodegradable dish soap
- ❏ Water bottle to carry while hiking
- ❏ Water jug to fetch water from the pump or faucet
- ❏ Food and drinks, remembering that you'll have only as much capacity to keep things cold as you have cooler space. You—and your children especially—will be sure to work up hearty appetites being outdoors all day, though, so pack a good amount of food, including any condiments/spices you like for cooking. Fresh fruit and vegetables are always good options as they are quick and need no refrigeration, as are things like granola bars and trail mix.
- ❏ Dog food if you're bringing a pet
- ❏ Dog bowls for food and water
- ❏ Dog leash
- ❏ Bags to pick up after your dog

Hike Index

About the Author

Melissa Watson is a professional firefighter and paramedic. An avid explorer with a passion for the outdoors, she has been camping, hiking, mountain biking, and photographing waterfalls and wildlife in the Carolinas for more than twenty-five years. From the mountains to the shore she is dedicated to the journey, and continually delves into new territory with a map and a compass in hand, a pack on her back, a camera at the ready, and her trusty dog Mikey by her side. Melissa has also written three other FalconGuide books: *Hiking Waterfalls in Georgia and South Carolina, Hiking Waterfalls in North Carolina,* and *Camping North Carolina.* You may find the waterfall guidebooks especially helpful as you venture out into the Upcountry of South Carolina. For more information, visit her website at trailtimenow.com, e-mail her at gypsyfool@aol.com, or send her a friend request on Facebook.

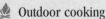
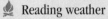
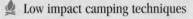